WISDOM FOR LIVING

Daily Bible Reading Notes

Martyn Perry

Martyn Perry

Wisdom For Living
Copyright © 2019 by Martyn Perry. All rights reserved

TABLE OF CONTENTS

Page 4   Introduction.
Page 5   The Twelve Minor Prophets.
Page 21   People Like Us.
Page 42   Jesus and the Cross.
Page 51   The Holy Spirit Brings….
Page 59   The Fruit of the Spirit.
Page 72   Worship.
Page 79   The Journey of Faith.
Page 87   God is….
Page 97   Acts 2:42.
Page 103 Living the Life.
Page 120 Seeking and Finding.
Page 124 A Selection of Prayers.
Page 130 Bibliography.

INTRODUCTION

God speaks to us in the Scriptures, His written Word. It is so important to spend time each day with God reading our Bibles and praying. When we do this, we are able to understand what He has said, and seek Him about what this might mean for us in our daily lives.

In this book, Wisdom for Living, we look together at some of the Scriptures. These include the Twelve Minor Prophets (Hosea to Malachi), the Sermon on the Mount (Matthew chapters 5-7), Acts 2 verse 42, and various Biblical themes, for example, Seeking and Finding, People Like Us, and Worship. Some prayers are also included at the end for those who find that helpful.

As we spend time looking at God's Word we will hear Him speaking into our lives in a way that only He can.

THE TWELVE MINOR PROPHETS

Hosea

Read Hosea 3:1-5

The Minor Prophets are "minor" not because they are unimportant, but because the books are short. By comparison with the Books of Isaiah, Jeremiah, and Ezekiel they certainly are. The Jewish community brought them together as a single collection called the Twelve. Short each one of them may be, but together they say a great deal to us about God and the life of the people of God, and that includes us.

Hosea tells us about how much God loves us. The prophet struggled with his feelings for his highly unfaithful wife. There is clearly a sense in which he understood how the God of Israel felt about the people of God, wayward as they often were. Hosea's wife, Gomer, returned to her old life as a prostitute at one of the shrines on the hilltops of Israel. So often it seemed that the people of God turned their backs on Him too, in order to give their attention and worship to Baal or one of the other gods of Canaan.

Hosea chapter 14 begins with an invitation to the people to return to their God and to be faithful to Him, for He had rescued them from slavery in Egypt in the first place. How good it is to know that God is as a gracious as that; He really is our Saviour.

There might have been times for us in our lives when we will have given our affection and attention to anything or anyone other than God. Life can be like that when there are a significant number of calls upon our time. It can be difficult sometimes to make God a priority and to decide to take our faith seriously. We can so easily find that we have been drifting away from Him.

When God invites us to return, we know that the invitation comes with a guarantee that we'll be accepted when we do. The One we read about in the Scriptures is gracious and loving to us. That's why the message we proclaims is called Good News. It certainly is.

Joel
Read Joel 2:21-27

We live in a world that is no stranger to calamity and disaster. It doesn't take us long watching the news or reading the paper to come up with a long list of ways in which people suffer and find life difficult. On occasion we know that a particular person is responsible; sometimes, however, it isn't as easy as that to understand why the suffering comes. It doesn't take long before we hear someone or other arguing that disaster struck because God was getting even with somebody.

Jesus wasn't hugely convinced by this way of thinking. That becomes clear when He heard people expressing the view that a person was born blind because of sin, or that a tower fell on top of a group because they were particularly sinful. The same was the case when He was told that a number of people from the north of the country in Galilee were murdered in the Temple in Jerusalem because God was getting even.

When the annual crop was blitzed by a swarm of locusts, about 400 years before the birth of Jesus, this was a disaster on a big scale for inhabitants in the land. Prosperity came with a good crop; real poverty came when the crop failed. Joel the prophet does seem to have seen this event in the light of judgement coming upon the people of God because of their sins. But he had more to say about it than that.

They would be able to worship once more, and to eat until their hunger was satisfied, because God would give them the kind of blessing in practice that would at least equal the disaster they had experienced. God longs to help and bless people; Joel was convinced of the fact. It's important that we remain unconvinced when we hear arguments to the contrary.

Amos
Read Amos 2:6-16

How easy we can find it to settle for something less than the whole truth. Of course, that's understandable because many of the problems we face are very complicated. A simple answer can sometimes reassure us. When we step beyond that, however, we become aware that reducing an international problem to victims and villains doesn't do justice to the situation. It can also be unjust to society's favourite villains or scapegoats.

Clearly, Amos had a real commitment to speaking out about injustice and oppression in his days. The poor were being treated badly, and God wasn't content to leave things as they were.

The greatness of this little book, however, lies in the fact that it is never simplistic and it has a commitment to using the same standard to judge everyone. There's criticism of Damascus, Gaza, Tyre, Edom, and everyone else in the region. The prophet then uses the same standard to criticize the lifestyle of the people of God (Judah and Israel). His commitment to the God of all truth meant that for him, the same standard needed to be used to understand and criticize everyone. Using this standard, he would certainly be critical of Judah and Israel—they wouldn't be let off the hook. But the book would end with words of comfort addressed specifically to them.

God is the God of all truth. When we become indifferent to it, we become indifferent to God. We only truly speak out in God's name when nothing less than the whole truth will do. In that, Amos shows us the way.

Obadiah

Read Obadiah verses 15 to the end

This little book may be brief, but it highlights a longstanding feud that caused much trouble for the nation of Judah. The feud was with a neighbouring tribe called Edom. We read about the start of all of the trouble in Genesis 25 when two brothers fell out, Jacob being the ancestor of Judah, Esau the ancestor of the Edomites. This falling out had repercussions for many years to come.

The writers of the various books of the Bible tell us that on the one hand, the two individuals made peace, yet on the other, their descendants were consumed by the feud which had been triggered back in the mists of time.

We hold these two pictures from Scripture together—the reconciliation between two individuals and the massive hostility between their descendants. As we do, we can perhaps call to mind examples from our own experience, when individuals patch up a quarrel, but their supporters never do. Sometimes this refusal to forgive is presented as if it were a virtue. We hear people claiming that had they been the wronged party, forgiveness would be possible, but they could never forgive what the alleged wrongdoer did to their relative or friend.

Truly, there is never anything noble about refusing to mend relationships. In Ephesians 4:26 we are told of the danger of carrying anger over to the next day. In reality, this can damage us more than it damages the person against whom we nurse the grudge. How easy it is for bitterness to grow in a heart that's toxic with the hatred of others.

Let's do all that we can to mend broken relationships. There's no time like the present. Let's also do all we can to make sure no one carries forward the hostility in our name.

Jonah
Read Jonah 4

One of the most important things in life is that we take seriously the call to become more holy. We come across this in Leviticus 19:2 when the people of God are taught about the importance of sharing the holy life of God. In 2 Peter 1:4 we hear again about our sharing in the nature of God.

As we become more and more like Him, with the divine nature growing within us, the call to holiness becomes an attractive thing, for we are sharing in nothing less than the beauty of God. If we understand the call to holiness in this way, we become the kind of people who want to include others in the life of God; grace has made holiness possible for us. How could we not want others to come to know our gracious God?

The book of Jonah underlines the fact that people from other nations were welcomed into the people of God. The desire to reach out to others said something about the nature of God too. In a way, Jonah, the prophet, is shown to be someone whose commitment to holiness meant that he wanted outsiders to be kept outside. This, however, was not the view of those who received this book into the Scriptures, for they understood God in a positive and attractive way.

No doubt we want to become more like God in our daily lives. That's obviously a good thing. Praying and reading the Scriptures will therefore be important to us in this. The fact that Jonah is part of God's message to us speaks so powerfully. The more like God we become, the more attractive our lives will be to others, and the more we will be on the lookout for positive ways to welcome others into the life of God. Holiness and mission go hand in hand.

Micah

Read Micah 6:1-8

The last verse of the book of Micah (7:20) tells us that God is always faithful to us; God's people can have a real assurance about that. It isn't that they are the people of God today, but that tomorrow they are thrown onto the scrap heap. God doesn't move on to love and accept others instead. Even if faithfulness is sometimes in short supply in our society, it defines God's dealings with us (2 Timothy 2:13). We can be sure it always will.

What isn't an option for us, though, is simply to celebrate the truth of God's faithfulness to us, and to treat others any way we like. God wants society to be imbued with that kind of consistent concern for all of its members.

This concern will happen, as God's teaching in Micah 6:8 is taken seriously; this must happen in practice not simply in theory. The prophets call us to a commitment to be fair in our dealings with everyone, to show mercy to others, even when they have wronged us, and to live with humility before God. In proclaiming this, the prophets are calling Israel back to the teaching God gave to Moses as found in the first five books of the Bible.

Of course, it is important to work for the kind of society, in which these qualities will be our guiding principles. However, that isn't intended to be the sum total of our calling as individuals. There will be times in our lives when we will be called to show practical kindness and help to people when this lies within our ability to deliver it. It isn't enough to identify a problem and to say "Someone should do something." This isn't "job done." If I can help in practice, I'm called to help in practice. Our faithful God hasn't asked anything less of me.

God will help us as we work for a godly society and world. He will help us, too, as we care for the neighbour who is closer to home.

Nahum

Read Nahum 1:12-2:2

When suffering comes to an end, all sorts of things can happen. Some of these might be understandable but they're not pretty. This is especially the case if the suffering in question was caused by others. Perhaps a dictator is finally toppled and those who are newly liberated destroy the dictator's image and settle scores with his former supporters.

The tiny state of Judah had long lived in the shadow of mighty Assyria; so had others. Assyria, the onetime regional superpower, eventually fell. We can only imagine the jubilation of those who had suffered at Assyria's hands. In Judah there were those who felt that God had had the final word concerning that powerful nation. Yet the prophets continued to call, in God's name, for Judah herself to deal with her own sins. It wasn't enough simply to crow about Assyria's downfall. Failing to repent sincerely, Judah would also soon cease to exist as a nation.

Our world is a complicated and turbulent place at times. It's all too easy for us to be made aware of the sins and crimes of others. In fact the media screams such things at us hour by hour. But in the light of this, the important thing for us is to reflect on our own lives and bring to God, in confession, those things that are amiss. Times such as these, spent with God, can be so important.

As we resist the temptation to rejoice over other people's sins (1 Corinthians 13:6) we, ourselves, can become the people God wants us to be. It's difficult for us to make progress on our journey to spiritual maturity, however, if gloating over other people's sins is one of our favourite pastimes. Getting rid of that habit is never a bad idea.

Habakkuk
Read Habakkuk 1:12-13

The Babylonians were by this time (c. 600 BCE) at the height of their power; they could do what they liked, and no one could stop them. They had done all manner of things to Lebanon to the north, and Habakkuk's anxiety knew no bounds as the Babylonians headed south towards the people of God. The tiny nation of Judah surely knew what was coming.

The prophet could do nothing but ask why God remained silent at all of this. God's people cried out, but there seemed to be no answer. How long (1:2) would God wait before acting? As we read through the book, however, we find that anxiety doesn't have the final word at all. The final section speaks to us about the importance of worshipping God. It's here we find that God is the One who gives strength (3:19), the Saviour who helps (verse 18).

One of the great things about Habakkuk is that he gives us an example of people being totally honest with God in prayer and worship. It's chiefly in worship that we, ourselves, are convinced that nothing is ultimately beyond God's control. When there are difficulties in our lives, the best thing we can do is to be faithful in worship.

In difficult times, worship is a real act of faith. It shows that we really do trust in God. Things are tough, but He is in charge and won't let us down. With this as one of our guiding principles, we can face any difficulty. Centuries later, the Letter to the Romans could affirm that those who are right with God live by faith (Habakkuk 2:4, Romans 1:17). When we can't understand what God is doing, we need to trust Him and to continue in worship. When we do this, we are able to receive all the strength that He wants to give.

Zephaniah
Read Zephaniah 3:11-20

How important it is to remain focussed when all sorts of things are going on. If we don't, we can easily drown in the detail of the many noisy and worrying things that are going on around us. The trick seems to be to remind ourselves of God's goodwill toward us, and of His determination to work everything out in line with His good purposes. This is especially important when things look bleak in the present.

Zephaniah ministered in Judah before the nation was finally overrun by Babylonian forces. His message, and that of the other prophets at the time, was that the nation needed to mend its sinful ways and turn to God. We can only imagine the frustration of those who brought this message to the people of God when there seemed to be few signs of it being heeded. Perhaps disaster would indeed strike. Either way, there was nothing the prophets could do to prevent it.

Yet these prophetic books often included positive material, even if the general situation seemed far from hopeful. A small number, a remnant, would eventually want to continue to be the people of God. They would be preserved and blessed by God.

One of Jesus' most brilliant followers, Paul, had the ability to look beyond his contemporary situation, with all of the suffering that the days brought for him. He was absolutely certain that God would ultimately work everything out for good (Romans 8:28). God's purposes would be worked out. And when we want to live in line with His purposes, we have every reason to live with confident hope.

If these are particularly difficult days for us, let's hold on to the goodness of God and the love He has for us. Without a shadow of doubt, we can again experience God's blessing in our lives. Let's live in the light of it.

Haggai
Read Haggai 1:1-6.

These days in the UK, the Law is rightly used to ensure that no one has to engage in dangerously excessive levels of work, week in week out. This is sensible; no-one wants to see tired people operating heavy machinery. Indeed, how often we lose our joy when we overwork.

Then, we can so easily feel that we are running on empty, and we can end up wondering how we can ever make it through the coming week.

When the Jewish people came back home after their enforced exile, they needed to make a start on getting their lives back on track. It seems that they put in a huge amount of effort. They planted crops and built houses of high quality, yet something seemed to be missing. They put in huge amounts of work, but seemed to have little to show for it. This can often happen when excessive work makes us lose hold of what really matters.

The Prophet Haggai knew what was missing. He noticed all the effort the people were making. And, truth to tell, their projects were important as they returned to their ancestral homeland. What was wrong was that they hadn't thought it a priority to rebuild the Temple, the place of worship, where they received God's forgiveness and grace. They decided it wasn't the right time to rebuild it, and that decision meant that they left God out of the picture. Their priorities and preferences became more important than God's will.

So very often we lose a sense of perspective when we feel that our short-term needs and desires are more important than living appropriately before God. It isn't even as if that way of life works or gives real peace.

When we make provision for the spiritual dimension of life, the rest can often work out too. Jesus said as much (Matthew 6:33). We can't do better than take our Lord's teaching seriously. His words are right in themselves, and His insights work in practice. Following Him also gives us real satisfaction day by day. Deciding to put God first is always wise. When we do, things so often seem to click into place.

Zechariah
Read Zechariah 1:16-17

Zechariah ministered to the returning exiles at around the same time as the Prophet Haggai. The Temple was to be rebuilt. God had comforted His people and had given them prosperity. There is a note of encouragement here as well, as God promises to protect and bless Judah (Zechariah 2:4-5).

As we live in faith and with genuine humility, there is something observable and tangible about the way God helps and blesses us. We noted yesterday, in the words of Jesus, that God gives us all of the good things we need in daily life (Matthew 6:33).

When a believer is living a spiritually attractive life, this can be such a powerful instrument in the hand of God, who wants other people to experience this grace for themselves. It isn't that we never make mistakes; neither is it that we don't struggle with things the way others do. The truth is, however, that we can have a sense of peace and joy about us when we know that the blessings of life come from God. God is the One who loves us, blesses us, and helps us in practice.

The people of God are described in Scripture (Matthew 5:14) as a city on a hilltop which shines its light on surrounding areas. We might be surprised how much of a positive effect our lives have on those around us as we live day by day. Let's pray for family members, friends, and work colleagues. Let's pray that our lives will send a positive message to them about the One who gave Himself for us.

Malachi
Read Malachi 2:13-16

We can't assume that after the ministries of Haggai and Zechariah, and the rebuilding of the Temple, God's people pleased Him in everything they did. That isn't the case, as Malachi makes clear. What God wanted, amongst other things, was that family life should flourish throughout the country. This would require attention too.

It's obviously right to underline the calling that some of us have to being single. After all, single people are part of family life. It's also important to make clear that there are times when getting divorced might be the appropriate way forward for us, especially if our marriages are dangerous, violent and abusive. As a rule, however, an easy-come easy-go attitude to marriage and divorce can destabilize society and be cruel beyond measure for the person who feels abandoned.

God cares about us and longs to help when we have been damaged in this way. He wants stable and loving families to be the place in which children grow up to become mature and godly adults themselves. When we have learnt good things about family life in our earlier years, this can be so helpful as we set out and establish families of our own.

If our own early experience of family life has been less than helpful, however, this doesn't mean that positive relationships will always elude us. We are not forever condemned to repeat the unhelpful things we might have picked up in early life. God can heal us of past hurts and is delighted when we pray about such things. Good things are possible, and He can help to bring them about.

PEOPLE LIKE US

Our Ancestors in Faith
Read Hebrews 11:1-7; 12:1-2

If we were asked to come up with lists of people who have had positive and negative influences on us in some way, I wonder who we'd choose. Almost certainly, it wouldn't take us long to complete the task. We can all think of those who have helped or harmed us over the years.

The writers of different parts of the Bible had their own reasons for preaching, praying, and writing as they did. They will have had particular things to say about God and how life should be lived. In addition to this, through the things they wrote, we can still find good advice which speaks into our situations.

In the Books of Kings, we're not simply given the bare bones of what happened in ancient Israel and Judah, and the dates of when things took place. In 1 and 2 Kings we're told about the kings who did what was pleasing to God and those who did the opposite. The writer of the Letter to the Hebrews was therefore in good company when, in chapter 11, he gave a list of Biblical heroes who had exercised faith in their lives. Hebrews is very much like a sermon in many ways, and it seems to have been addressed to Jewish believers who might have been going through particularly difficult times. In effect, they were being encouraged to learn from the good example of their ancestors who lived by faith and trusted God even when things were difficult.

As we live our lives, it is important that we try to give a good example to those who might notice the things we're doing and saying. Of course, as human beings we are affected by things we hear. The truth is, however, that we learn even more effectively from the things we see. Things we say can have an effect on others; but the positive example of a life lived for God can be even more effective. Let's pray that we might one day be remembered by someone who came to faith, or persevered in it, because of our example.

Abraham and Sarah

Read Genesis 12:1-9

Many millions of people in our world look back to Abraham and Sarah and consider them their ancestors in the faith. In Genesis we're told that God asked Abraham to leave everything that he was familiar with and set out on a journey. God didn't even give him details of the destination at that stage. It takes a great deal of faith to set out on a journey like that.

Though Abram and Sarai, as they were known at first, found that journeying with God would ask a lot of them, their sense of being called kept them going. How much can be achieved when people trust God even if they can't always see the whole picture at the outset. This good and positive example inspires us to trust God and to attempt great things for Him; if Abraham and Sarah can accomplish great things for God, so can we.

If we were to read the rest of Genesis 12, however, we would notice that these two people of faith didn't always get things right. The situation in which they found themselves, at this stage of their journey, seemed to be fraught with danger. There was clearly a limit to the amount of faith in God they could muster. So Abraham and Sarah decided to try to work things out for themselves rather than rely on the Lord. For a while, they seem to have left God out of the picture, and trouble followed. It tends to.

Have we ever taken the wrong turning on our journey of faith? Perhaps we can understand how it feels to decide that we just have to work things out for ourselves. How good it is to know that when we decide to trust God once more and to resume our journey, He will be there for us and will lead us on. God uses people like Abraham, Sarah, you, and me. Wherever we are on our journey of faith at the moment, we can trust God to lead us forward in the right way. He is the best guide we could ever have.

Joseph
Read Genesis 50:15-21

Sometimes we hear people being referred to as "wise beyond their years." This indicates that they have a real measure of maturity early on in life. When we think of others, however, the truth is that, in the area of maturity, they are late developers. For them, early years are perhaps marked by the kind of impetuosity that will need to be dealt with in later life in order for stability and spiritual fruitfulness to grow.

Joseph was something of a late developer when it came to wisdom. His story starts in Genesis 37. In these early chapters we find him speaking impetuously and foolishly in the presence of his family, blabbing the content of dreams that he might have been wiser to have kept to himself. This helped to set in motion a chain of events that would see his brothers, who thoroughly disliked him by this stage, telling their father that Joseph was dead. In reality, he had been taken to Egypt by traders and sold into slavery.

The story came full circle as Joseph became a wise and hugely capable person who rose to high office in Egypt. By this stage he was astute enough to see that God was at work early on in his life, and had been over the years. Genesis chapter 50 verse 20 puts it beautifully; God was able to take the evil things Joseph's brothers did to him, and use them so that good things could come of them.

If we are wise beyond our years, we will no doubt already have come to realize the extent to which God is active in our lives. Yet for those of us who are late developers, we often need a little encouragement and reassurance about this. What is crucial is that we don't dwell on the mistakes we might have made in earlier life but allow God to use us now and in the future. God can give us the wisdom that we need, as He tells us in James 1:5. As we come to see God at work in our lives, we will no doubt realize that He has been working things out for us from early years. God uses us, even in spite of ourselves at times. We can always thank Him for that.

Moses

Read Exodus 2:11-15a

Well, this doesn't seem like a very good start for a man who was to become a towering figure in the life of the Jewish community. Moses would become the one who would teach the children of Israel so much about the holiness of God. He would end up understanding a great deal about how to live life before God, how to shape society, and how to worship Him appropriately. The five books Moses wrote, the ones at the beginning of the Bible, are so wonderful.

As we read through the first few chapters of Exodus, we find Moses to be a person who had, perhaps, an overdeveloped confidence in his own ability, and an underdeveloped sense of what God could do through him. Yet, he was precisely the person God called to teach and lead the Israelites.

In our world, we often admire people who are naturally gifted and can get things done. This isn't always a bad thing, of course, especially when we see our natural abilities as God given. Proverbs 3:5 is so wise, however. It asks us to rely on God rather than solely on our understanding of things. Moses would come to rely on God in a wonderful way. In the later chapters of Exodus, he is even shown discussing everything with Him. How far Moses had travelled.

Not even the most intelligent person can understand everything completely, when they rely on their own ability. We are wise, at those times, to rely on God, for He understands everything. Praying about things can be the wisest thing we ever do. When we don't, we can easily end up making decisions that seem right to us in the short term only. Then, as we look back, the flaws in our thinking become apparent. We would have been wiser to have taken more time and to have talked to God about the decisions we needed to take. Time spent in prayer is never time wasted. It is always good to talk to God. He sees and understands everything.

Joshua

Read Joshua 1:1-9

Pride isn't a lovely characteristic. It doesn't help us form great and lasting friendships. How could it? When we're proud, everything about us is, too—our ability, our opinions, our likes, and our dislikes. Humility, by contrast, helps us to think about others. It helps us become the kind of person others seek out; in the presence of a humble person, others matter too. Perhaps it is for this reason we read in Scripture that God opposes the proud and gives grace to those who are humble (Proverbs 3:34; James 4:6; 1 Peter 5:5).

In the first five books of the Bible (called "the Torah," or "the Teaching," by the Jewish community), we encounter Joshua as the one who helps Moses. He doesn't try to topple or replace the older leader. He knows what God had asked him to do and gets on with it. Indeed, the Book of Joshua begins by still referring to him as Moses' assistant.

After the death of the great teacher, however, the younger man would lead the people of God as they struggled to find a place where they could feel at home. This would be a place where they could live the holy life about which Moses had taught. Joshua was moving from preparation for leadership to leadership in practice, and he was ready to make that change.

Preparation can be crucial if we want to succeed in things God asks us to do. When we start to get a sense that God might be leading us in a particular direction, rushing at it can be a real danger. Time spent in preparing for things is the key. Perhaps God has asked us to be involved in doing relatively undemanding things so far. This might not mean that that's how things are always going to be. If we are faithful and consistent in doing the things people tend not to notice, it might be that we will be in the right place to do more demanding things for God later on. Joshua found that for himself. We might too.

Hannah and Samuel
Read 1 Samuel 1:1-18

The birth of Samuel, about which we read in 1 Samuel 1:19-28, took place in ancient Israel when polygamy was not unheard of. His father, Elkanah, had two wives, Peninnah and Hannah. We read that Peninnah had children but Hannah did not. It was against this background that Hannah prayed for children at the shrine which they visited every year. Eventually Samuel was born, and he was given to God so that he could serve Him for the whole of his life. He became a prophet who would play a significant role in the history of the tribes of God.

The birth of every child is special, of course, yet Scripture often sees something particularly significant in the birth of those who are set apart to do certain things for God. Later on in the Bible, we read of the call of the great Prophet Jeremiah (Jeremiah 1). God knew him even before he was born and set him apart for this special ministry.

Concerning the birth of our Saviour, Jesus, we read that this has the highest possible significance (Matthew chapters 1 and 2; Luke chapters 1 and 2). Indeed, the song of praise of Mary, the mother of Jesus (Luke 1:46-55), is remarkably similar to that of Hannah after the birth of Samuel (1 Samuel 2:1-10).

The things we do for God don't come as a surprise to our Creator. He knew us even before we were born. This makes us, and everyone else, special. Certainly, the good things we have done are highly valued by the God who knows us by name and knew the choices we would make even before we did.

This being so, it is right to thank Him for our lives and for the things that He has helped us to achieve. We know that we are important to our Creator, who guides us through life. This is a wonderful truth; it encourages us to know that He holds us in the palm of His hand. We can certainly thank Him for that.

David and Bathsheba
Read 2 Samuel 11:1-5

Many years before this dreadful incident took place, Samuel had anointed David to be King of Israel, and eventually, after the death of Saul, he was enthroned. There was so much that was impressive about this man that his reign, and that of Solomon who succeeded him, would be considered a golden age for the people of God.

Having said this, there was much in his life that God would need to forgive; breaking the commandments doesn't get more serious than adultery and murder. We can only guess at Bathsheba's complicity in these events. In ancient times when women will have had much less power than men, we shouldn't easily assume that guilt attaches to her at all. How could she say "No" to the King? Truth to tell, Bathsheba may have been something of a victim. After all, it was to the King that the Prophet Nathan would later go to announce responsibility and guilt; he was the man.

We pray that we may know nothing, ourselves, of serious sin. Yet there may still be things on the road to adultery and murder with which we need God's help. The teaching of Jesus gets to the root of the matter. He spoke about the first steps we take along this path and the importance of coming to terms with them (Matthew 5:22, 28). Anger and lust are highly corrosive and can't be allowed to grow unchecked in us. God can help us overcome them; that is part of the Good News.

If we take the call to holiness seriously, making progress ourselves in this area is much more constructive than spending time denouncing the sins of others. When we give in to a lynch-mob mentality and yell at other people, this can easily be designed to try to drown out what we know of our own sins: "I might have done this, but I've never done that." May God help us to walk the way of holiness ourselves rather than take this spiritual cul de sac.

Solomon

Read 1 Kings 3:16-28

However awful our sins might be, God's grace can bring about repentance and a new beginning. David and Bathsheba became the parents of Solomon, and he was a most impressive and wise King of Israel.

Solomon was a person who was associated with wisdom by God's people, in the same way that his father, David, was with music and praise. Today's reading gives a spectacular example of what wisdom could look like in practice. This gift from God allowed him to understand what people were like and how things work. There is something impressive and down to earth about a spirituality which is immersed in wisdom. The Book of Proverbs gives us such a wonderful example of that. Wisdom, articulated by Solomon, describes how it is possible to please God in all of the ordinary things of life.

It's in the ordinary things that we can please God and live out a holy life. We don't despise the demands and opportunities of the day and think that purely religious and spiritual things are what really interest God. If we were to see things that way, we'd end up seeing other people, and ordinary things, as an intrusion.

Far from being that, they are the opportunities that God gives to live a genuinely spiritual life. When this kind of wisdom finds a home within us, it's precisely in the next conversation, email reply, Tweet or text sent that we can serve God.

Wisdom helps us see the diary, the kitchen calendar, and the In-box as holy things. That being so, I wonder how we can serve God today?

Ezra and Nehemiah
Read Nehemiah 6:15-16, 8:18

These verses describe some of the work that the Jewish people had to do in order to rebuild their community when their leaders were freed from enforced exile far away from home. When they returned to the Holy Land, there was so much to do.

The Temple in Jerusalem had been destroyed, and the walls around the city had been breached. The people could know nothing by way of day to day safety until the walls were rebuilt. In addition to this, there would need to be something of a serious engagement with the ancient Scriptures of Israel so that they could begin to organize their lives in a way that would be pleasing to God. Had they done only one of the two, life would have been lacking security or spiritual stability.

It was for this reason that God sent both Nehemiah and Ezra to the city. Nehemiah would be responsible for rebuilding the walls, and Ezra would teach the people about God as He was revealed in the Scriptures.

God wants us to be safe and secure in life. If we are not, it's difficult to build the kind of communities that He wants to see. Unless this goes hand in hand with a genuine and healthy spiritual renewal, however, life will be thin at best. It is important that we try to take both of these things seriously, as we take decisions for ourselves that will have a good and positive impact on our lives. Mature people see the importance of the decisions they take, for these always come with consequences attached.

It's also good to pray for those who lead us in various parts of our national life. Decisions they take on our behalf affect so many people. Let's not forget, we're asked to include our leaders when we pray for others (1 Timothy 2:1-4). It's important that we as individuals, communities, and nations take responsible decision making seriously. When this happens, all sorts of good things become possible

Esther

Read Esther 4:1-14

Over very many centuries, the Jewish people have looked to God for help during times of dreadful suffering. The Biblical Feast of Passover celebrates rescue from slavery in Egypt. Each year the story is retold and God is worshipped.

Today's reading comes from a book which tells of the Feast of Purim and the God who saves. Mordecai is described as a godly man who served in the court of King Ahasuerus at Susa. His relative, Esther, had become Queen, and both were members of the people of God far away from their ancestral home. All was not well, however, as another official at the court, the villain Haman, came to take a strong dislike to Mordecai. As the story unfolds, Haman tricks the King into implementing a plan to put the Jewish community to death throughout the Empire.

These verses tell of Mordecai's response. He had come to the conclusion that Esther had become Queen precisely so that she could beg the King for the safety of her people, even though this was a dangerous course to take. The book comes to a close with this annual feast of celebration being agreed upon by the people. Though God isn't actually mentioned throughout the story, the One who saves is truly the central character. He is a very active player in all of this.

It is right for the people of God to give thanks for the blessings of the past. So many festivals in the Jewish and Christian calendars do just that. If we celebrate God's acts of redemption appropriately, however, we find that we don't live in the past in an unhelpful way. Instead, we are given strength to meet the challenges of the present and to plan for the future with confidence and humility. The One who has acted in the past does so today and can be relied upon in time to come. It's always good to celebrate a God like this.

Ruth

Read Ruth 1:1-14

Ruth was a convert. It was following the death of her husband that this woman from Moab decided to accompany her mother-in-law, Naomi, as she returned to Judah. The words which speak of her decision to join the people of God are amongst some of the most beautiful that we find anywhere in Scripture. Ruth says to Naomi: "Intreat me not to leave thee, or to return from following after thee: for whither thou goest, I will go; and where thou lodgest, I will lodge: thy people shall be my people, and thy God my God" (Ruth 1:16, KJV).

It was out of sadness and loss that Ruth turned to God. So much in life depends on how we react to things. It is strange that calamity can strike two people and the end result can be very different.

There are some sad times in life that, as far as we can tell, seem to bring a person's spiritual life to an end. They wonder why God has decided to bring misfortune their way. Yet at the same time, there are those who make a commitment to God, and convert during times of sadness. Their testimony is that they could never have got through their difficulty without God's help.

This book is in Scripture partly to underline the importance of God's people welcoming converts. It also asks us how we react when sadness comes our way. If these are particularly difficult days for us, being real with God and praying honestly can be crucially important. This doesn't make everything O.K. overnight, of course, but it does mean that we are in a position to receive the comfort God longs to give. Let's not struggle on in our own strength. God wants to be there for us, and prayer can make this a reality.

Jacob
Read Genesis 32:22-32

Some families are dysfunctional with relationships between the different members that leave a lot to be desired. There are times when we notice that even against the odds, children with an incredibly difficult upbringing manage to form good and helpful relationships in families of their own. Mistakes don't always have to be repeated down the years from one generation to the next. Even when we do find ourselves doing the very things we vowed not to, God can help, and relationships can be repaired.

As we read Scripture, we see our great ancestors in the faith doing all sorts of unhelpful things at times. A case in point would be Jacob, his brother Esau, and their parents, Isaac and Rebekah. Each parent favoured a different son, and between the four of them we find excellent examples of cheating, deceit, and using others to fulfil one's own plans. And, yes, Jacob, when he became a parent, would have his own favourite son too (Genesis 37:3).

If ever there was a plot for a biblical soap opera, this was it. Yet, even with all of this being acted out, we also see in the story a desire to restore relationships even though they had seemed to have fractured beyond repair. Jacob and Esau would eventually make peace. This can encourage us to dare to believe that God can create something that speaks of forgiveness and grace even in some of the most awful situations.

In all of this, we also find Jacob wrestling with God in a way that would change him forever. He would no longer principally be known as the one who had cheated his brother. He would be known as the one who had struggled against God and had received His blessing. God specializes in working with unpromising material and achieving more than would ever have been thought possible.

Josiah
Read 2 Kings 22:8-11

Kings of Judah who were Josiah's predecessors left a lot to be desired. By comparison with them, however, Josiah had a real commitment to the God who had rescued them from slavery in Egypt. We see this in his response to hearing God's Word through the reading of an ancient book which had just been discovered in the Temple.

Many Biblical scholars think that the "Book of the Law" which had been found in the Temple was, in fact, the book we know as Deuteronomy. This seems likely due to the significant overlap between the document which was discovered and the steps the King took having heard it read for the first time. Its message was clear: blessing would follow a whole-hearted commitment to God; rejection of God would be a serious matter for the entire nation.

What had begun as a visit to the Temple to arrange for repair work on the building, ended in a programme of reform to the life of the whole country. The shrines to other deities would need to be removed; God alone would be worshipped in Judah, and this would take place in the Temple in Jerusalem. Josiah had heard God's Word; he knew he should act upon it.

God doesn't ask us to be impetuous, but some things are so serious that it would be negligent to let a dangerous state of affairs drag on. When God speaks to us, it can often be important to take advice from a wise and godly person. That's exactly what the King did after the Book of the Law was read to him (2 Kings 22:11-20). The wisdom of someone we rightly trust can be helpful, as, indeed, can their prayers. When we are asked to do things for God, we will need help and support. Going it alone can put us and others at risk.

Gideon

Read Judges 6:11-18

Every generation has issues with which it needs to grapple. In our days, perhaps we are particularly aware of the danger of glorifying war; that's not surprising after the bloodletting of the Twentieth Century. We are right to be aware of these things. However, as we look back to earlier times and find things that grate, people in the future will no doubt look back at our generation and see our shortcomings.

For this reason when we read material from a distant age, we need to have an understanding of the things with which people had to struggle then. The truth is that for ancient Hebrews looking for a home, had they not survived at the point of a sword, they would have perished at the point of a sword. There was no alternative. Leaders will have been chosen bearing this in mind.

Gideon was one such warrior-leader. His tribe, Manasseh, was locked in conflict with the Midianites. Desperate times required a particular kind of leader, and Gideon was that leader. When it came to sins and shortcomings, however, he seems to have had something approaching a full set. Perhaps for this reason he was well aware of his weaknesses. He wondered how God could ever use him.

Did the angel that greeted him have an overdeveloped sense of humour when he greeted Gideon as a mighty warrior? He felt like anything but that. Yet, it was to be the presence of God with him that would make the difference. With God's help he could do things that he could never achieve on his own. Gideon's tribe would find safety, and he would help to provide it.

It isn't a bad thing to be aware of our shortcomings. Allowing them to limit what we achieve in life is, however. God can help us to overcome all that is less than helpful in us. With God's help we are more than able to conquer our demons (Romans 8:37) and move beyond the things in our past.

Isaiah

Read Isaiah 6:1-13

These were difficult days for the people of God in Judah. Even though Israel, to the north, had already been overrun, Judah seemed to be arrogant and overconfident. The political skies in the region were growing ever darker, but Judah didn't seem to want to hear what God had to say. Regardless of choices they made, they thought everything would be O.K.

Who would want to minister to a country in these circumstances? Hopefully not a person who was equally arrogant and overconfident. We hear of Isaiah's acceptance of this difficult brief in today's reading. He was in the Temple, and certainly he seems to have been very familiar with what went on there. It was there that he had a sense of the holiness of God. This gave him not only an understanding of the sinfulness of the people, but also of his own sins too.

When we identify with those around us and have a sense of our own need of grace, this is the best possible launch pad for doing what God has asked us to do. Overconfidence and brazenness in the people of God is an unappealing thing, especially when this expresses itself in pronouncements about what others should do, presumably to join us on the moral high ground. In another part of Scripture, we have Daniel identifying with his people as he prays, "We have sinned" (Daniel 9:5).

The life we live before God is a celebration of grace. It can't very well be anything else if we have a realistic appreciation of who we are, and who God is. We are called to live as those who understand that forgiven people live as those who experience His grace day by day (Ephesians 2:8-10).

One More Thing
Read Genesis 1:1 and John 3:16

As we read about the experiences of our ancestors in the faith, a picture emerges of the kind of God we worship and follow. The God of Scripture is anything but distant. Having created all things, the Creator is active within the created order. His fingerprints are seen on so many things.

In the Scriptures God is shown to be involved with individuals, communities, nations and empires. The coming of Jesus shows exactly how involved God is. Our experience of Him is of One who understands us and wants the best for us. When we realize that He wants the best for us, however, we would be wrong to imagine that He wants the worst for others. There should be nothing sectarian or unhelpfully narrow about us when we learn to appreciate and experience God's love.

How wonderful that we take our place amongst the people of God, past, present, and future. We are part of the story of God accepting and forgiving people just as they, and just as we, are. Grace encourages us to come to repentance and to move on in the strength we receive from

His Spirit. Our calling is to worship, to grow in maturity, to respond to the needs of others, and to care for the world as those who work with God. Believing that we participate in God's life here and in heaven (2 Peter 1:4) doesn't make us indifferent to this world and those who share it with us.

God calls, equips, and uses people like us. What a privilege. The truth of this should never cease to amaze us.

JESUS AND THE CROSS

Words of Forgiveness
Read Luke 23:32-34

The Romans were skilled at many things. In particular, they had significant skill at putting criminals and troublemakers to death on the cross. This no doubt came with practice. Rome crucified very many thousands. There is nothing sacred in itself about being crucified, many were. What makes us attach so much significance to the Cross of Jesus is the nature of the One who was nailed to it.

The imperial authorities crucified Jesus in order to try to make sure that this charismatic Rabbi from Galilee didn't become the focus for more unrest than He already had. In Jerusalem during Passover, things could easily have turned ugly, with Jesus having entered the city like a King. Jerusalem would have been creaking at the seams because of the number of members of the Jewish community who had come to worship at the Temple. For the Romans, it was better to be safe than sorry. And Jesus, Himself, wasn't naïve when He went up to Jerusalem for the feast; He knew what to expect and embraced His calling.

When people wrong us or are cruel to us, forgiveness isn't the first thing we think of. If we follow Jesus with any degree of seriousness, however, forgiving others isn't an optional extra. It's part of what we are called to do. When we pray like Jesus did, we ask God to forgive others. As we pray for those who have hurt us, God can give us the grace and strength we need to really forgive. Releasing others sets us free too. As someone has said, refusing to forgive is like drinking poison ourselves in the hope of making the other person ill.

What we know in practice, however, is that the deeper our wounds are, the longer it can be before we can bring ourselves to release others in this way. This might be a journey we are making even now. As we ask God to go on healing us, we can come to that point of choosing to forgive. Sometimes we receive healing bit by bit. It might also be bit by bit that we come to forgive someone who has hurt us more than words can say. God understands how difficult things can be. Forgiveness is never an easy matter; that's why Jesus went to the Cross.

Reaching Out
Read Luke 23:39-43

When we are focussing almost exclusively on ourselves, due to illness or some problem, other people and their needs often fade into the background or disappear altogether. Perhaps you have helped to nurse a "bad patient" or have been forced to listen to someone who only wants to talk incessantly about themselves. It's as if nobody else exists or has real needs.

If ever a person could be forgiven for shutting others out and summoning all their strength just to cope, it would surely be someone on a cross. We can't begin to imagine the horror of being in such a situation. How telling that even there on the cross, Jesus was aware of others and their needs, especially their need to receive an assurance of the forgiveness of sin. One of the thieves crucified with Him recognized something about Him and reached out in his need to Jesus.

The response Jesus gave, that today the thief would be in paradise, says so much to us about how we can respond in our times of need, with God's help. When times are hard, it's understandable that a coping mechanism should be activated, as we turn in on ourselves and concentrate all of our resources on getting through this ordeal. As we turn to God, instead, we find that His grace can help (Hebrews 4:14-16). It might just be that as we cope with our illness or difficulty, with God's help, we'll be in the right place to reach out to others in their time of need, whatever their need might be.

Completed

Read John's Gospel 19:29-30

Words like "It is finished" could, in reality, mean any number of things. They could indicate that something is over and has ended in ruin. Here, as he records the words of Jesus, John conveys something altogether different. As this particular Gospel describes the crucifixion, Jesus is said to have been lifted up in glory so that others might be drawn to Him. There are sacrificial overtones here, too, for the early verses of the Gospel referred to Him as the Lamb of God. Now death is near and Jesus' mission comes to completion and fulfilment. "It is finished" is understood in this sense; Jesus' work is fully accomplished.

Though there is nothing glib or triumphalistic about John's presentation of Jesus, we are intended here to understand that our salvation is a completed act; we are expected to live in the light of it. Chapter 20 comes to an end by driving the matter home (verse 31); the Gospel has been written so that, believing in Him, we may have life. In the First Letter of John, this is spelt this out clearly (5:13); we are intended to know that we have eternal life.

This isn't an invitation to arrogance. Arrogance has to do with believing that we are basically more wonderful than others, and it's our mission to make that fact known. What John invites us to exhibit in daily life is confidence in God's grace and in what was accomplished in the life, ministry, and death of Jesus.

Though we'll never understand it all fully in this world, we can live as those who have begun to experience a quality of life that even death can't extinguish. This quality of life is in God's gift, and we have received it because Jesus went to the Cross for us. This can give us a holy joy (1 John 1:4). God wants us to live as those who have nothing less.

Into God's Safe Keeping.
Read Luke 23:44-46

The ancient monastic Office of Compline, or Night Prayer, echoes Psalm 31:5: "Into Your hands I commit my spirit; You have redeemed me, God of truth." It is a great thing to pray towards the end of the day as we prepare to sleep.

This was also something that was on the lips of Jesus before He took His last breath. In many ways, the answer to this prayer was found in the awesome fact of the empty tomb, just a few days later. The whole of His life had been an offering to God; His bodily resurrection would be God's spectacular announcement that the offering had been accepted.

Prayer was a natural part of the life and ministry of Jesus. How could it have been any other way when He lived as a member of the Jewish community, and worshipped every Sabbath at the synagogue in Nazareth? Prayer wasn't out of place, therefore, when He was dying on the Cross. What Jesus models for us is the reality of prayer as a moment by moment awareness of the presence of His Heavenly Father. This is part of the birthright of Jesus' followers, also, as we live in the power of the Holy Spirit. Prayer isn't simply something we do, in a way it's something we are.

Jesus didn't glide effortlessly through life as One who seemed to be human but wasn't really. We don't glide effortlessly through life either. It's for that reason that we need to pray following the example of Jesus. How we are invited to live is put beautifully in 1 Peter 5:7 as we are told that we can cast all our cares on God, because He cares for us. Let's ask the Holy Spirit to help us live in the reality of this. It's how Jesus lived, died and rose again; as His brothers and sisters, we can pray like this too.

Forsaken?

Read Matthew 27:45-46

It isn't a sin to doubt. Doubting is part of our human experience. In a sense, we can find it hard to trust God when we don't understand what's going on. Our grief and perplexity can be such that we wonder what God is doing or even whether He cares. Then, momentary doubt replaces trust in Him.

King David in Psalm 22 certainly seems to have reached that point. In the first half of the Psalm, before the problem had resolved itself, he couldn't imagine what was going on. That Jesus found this Psalm on His lips when He suffered on the Cross indicates that there are times when it can be quite proper for a person of faith to wonder whether God has abandoned them. It may be understandable to stop short of this level of honesty, but the more Biblical way, in our darker moments, is to tell God how bleak we feel.

Of course God always knows how we feel. To pray the opposite doesn't fool God, but it does make it harder to work our way through the grief, or sense of loss, and come out the other side truly knowing that all is well. Honesty and faith are not mutually exclusive. Honesty can, in fact, be an expression of faith, because it acknowledges that even if we don't know, God does and is happy to receive our prayer.

The psalmist would come through the difficulty and would be able to affirm that God rules and is mighty (Psalm 22:28). Our Lord Himself experienced the grave, but He also experienced the empty tomb. Paul is another example of a person who was well acquainted with suffering and real personal danger; his affirmation of confidence in God (Romans 8:18) was all the more realistic for his honesty. Telling God how we feel is an act of faith; it is also an affirmation on our part that we continue to believe that He does all things well.

Relationships
Read John's Gospel 19:25-27

As God's people, we are not simply called to affirm a set of beliefs. What we believe is important, of course, and much time is devoted to the subject in the Letters written by those who led the people of God in the First Century CE. However, we are called to live out what we believe, in our relationships with others. It is for this reason that we read in 2 John (verses 1-6) about knowing the Truth, and loving one another; truth and love are meant to go hand in hand.

In an earlier chapter, the Gospel of John will have told us that Jesus, Himself, is the fullness of Truth (14:6). In today's reading we find our Lord describing the relationship between His mother and John, one of His rabbinic disciples. It will be as they relate as mother and son that they will truly continue to celebrate the life to which God had called them. It isn't an option for the people of God to be strong on truth and weak on love. The opposite is equally unconvincing. We are on the right lines when we affirm what is true and truly love those whom God has put around us.

Jesus was approaching death. In various ways, Mary and John will have been in need of a comfort that only God could give. It would be given as each met the needs of the other; the relationship of mother and son would require nothing less of them.

We fulfil the words of Jesus when we care in practice for those God has brought into our sphere of influence. We are called to believe in the Lord and to love others as He commanded. (1 John 3:23). These are hallmarks of the true disciple. When we believe, we stand at the Cross in adoration; when we love others, we find Him in the needs of others. It's a privilege to believe in Him; it's also a privilege to care for those around us and to carry out His command.

I'm Thirsty.
Read John's Gospel 4:13-14; 19:28

On the Cross, in the heat of the day, Jesus fulfilled Scripture (Psalm 69:21) by saying that He was thirsty. This wouldn't have been the first time that our Lord admitted that He needed something that only someone else could give; He was fully human after all.

Earlier in His ministry, Jesus was travelling from Judea back home to Galilee in the north. He chose to travel through Samaria; this led Him into potentially hostile territory, because of the longstanding feud between the Samaritan and Jewish communities. As He passed through, He stopped at a well and asked a woman who had come to draw water for a drink because He was thirsty. He needed a drink; only she could supply it. Conversation developed quickly between the two, as we read in John 4. The exchange would end with her admitting her need. Hers was a need that only Jesus could supply—the living water of the Holy Spirit.

Very often we are more comfortable meeting the needs of others than in admitting that we have needs of our own. When we admit we lack something, this makes us just a little vulnerable. In a sense, we place ourselves in the hands of others; will they help or not? The example of Jesus invites us into this territory, even though it might make us feel challenged and weak.

In a society like ours, it's much easier to pretend that everything is O.K. with us; we are the ones who give to those who are less fortunate. As we follow the example of Jesus, however, the circle can be completed, and fellowship can be created. We care for others; they care for us. In this way, we take others seriously and remove the possibility that our gifts can be all about us. Jesus shows us a better way.

THE HOLY SPIRIT BRINGS...

Peace

Read John's Gospel 20:19-29

Life is busy. Perhaps it always was. The way we organize ourselves these days does, however, makes it particularly difficult to escape from the busyness we create for ourselves. Our mobiles, personal planners, and Inboxes can be a mixed blessing. It's no surprise, therefore, that when we want to find an oasis of peace in all of this, it can seem so elusive.

As we read through John's Gospel, we find Jesus offering to give those who believe in Him the kind of peace that can't be found anywhere else (14:27). In today's reading in John chapter 20, we find the risen Jesus appearing to His disciples. He breathed on them and gave them the Holy Spirit. They would need the Spirit if people were to encounter Jesus in and through their lives.

In these verses we find the gift of peace emphasized, too, as "Peace be with you" is repeated. Repetition of a word or phrase seems to be one of the ways John emphasizes that something important is at stake.

The risen Jesus wants His followers to have peace and to live in the reality of it because He has given the Spirit to them.

Peace, in the Holy Spirit, is for each of us. It isn't reserved for a few special people who stumble on a technique for dealing with life's anxieties. Peace becomes ours as we welcome God into the ordinary things we do; we live in the reality of God's peace especially as we make time for Scripture and prayer. When we do this, we receive God's grace and help.

Let's give God time as we read the Scriptures and prayerfully reflect on them. Though it can always be a temptation for us in our busyness to "read and go," time spent delighting in the presence of God can be crucial. As we pause, Jesus greets us, and the Spirit of God makes His peace a reality in our lives.

Confidence
Read Acts 2:1-4

For the group of timid disciples who huddled together in the days before the Jewish feast of Pentecost, or Shavuot, the gift of the Holy Spirit would make all the difference. One of the many things the Spirit brought them was an assurance that God had accepted and forgiven them. They had lacked confidence, towards the end of Luke's Gospel. In Acts, we see that confidence would now be present in abundance in their lives because of the Spirit.

In their various writings, early leaders amongst the people of God reflected this: Timothy needn't be timid (2 Timothy 1:7); God's children shouldn't be filled with fear (1 John 4:17-18); Jewish believers in Jesus could be certain that God would help them (Hebrews 4:16); believers were to be assured of their acceptance by God, which is why the Spirit was given in the first place (Ephesians 1:13-14).

God wants us to have real assurance that we are forgiven. Our present and future needn't be limited by what we have done in the past. God graciously assures us that everything we have thought, said, or done in the past is included in the forgiveness that is ours. Nothing, absolutely nothing, stands outside of it, regardless of what the devil might try to mutter to us from time to time.

The writer of Psalm 103 tells us that our sins have been removed from us as far as the east is from the west (verse 12). The Holy Spirit brings this assurance to us. As we reflect on the truth of it, God intends that we should forgive ourselves too. It is vital that we don't go on beating ourselves up for things the Lord has completely forgiven. Our lives are intended to be a celebration of the reality of our right standing with our Heavenly Father. This doesn't make us arrogant, but it does give us many reasons to rejoice in Him.

Power.

Read Isaiah 40:25-31 and Ephesians 6:10

Judah's leaders were in Exile after their nation had been overrun by the Babylonians. The poor were left behind to till the land; the leaders were in Exile and no longer able to lead the people. As they contemplated a return home, the picture for leaders and people alike was one of powerlessness. These beautiful verses from Isaiah speak of God being able to renew His people and give them the strength they needed for the task ahead. They were powerless, but they would be empowered as they trusted in Him. These words, written at a much earlier date, would nevertheless have supplied them with confidence as they prepared to move back to their ancestral homeland.

Centuries later, those who trusted in Jesus were well aware of the spiritual difficulties they faced. Life felt like a battle; if they relied solely on their own resources, they would hardly be equal to the challenge. In the Letter to the Ephesians (6:10), they were reassured that help was at hand. They would be able to withstand whatever came their way in the strength of God's power.

It's good to know that God never asks us to do things that are beyond us. The Holy Spirit brings His resources to us, and in practice that makes all the difference. When we feel weary and faint, as the people of God did in Exile, our strength can be renewed by the Spirit.

We are not given power so that we can control others and make them do what we want, in any area of life. The power the Spirit brings enables us to serve God and others in His name. Peter and John brought wholeness and healing to someone in need as they went to the Temple to worship. We read about this in Acts 3:1-10. God is delighted when we make a positive difference to people's lives in the strength the Spirit gives. It is for this reason that we are empowered by the One who responds to our prayers with extravagant generosity.

Fellowship.
Read 1 John 4:11-13

The Holy Spirit doesn't share God's resources with us so that we can go it alone without our spiritual brothers and sisters. He doesn't equip us so that we can make a name for ourselves. We are not meant to act as though we alone are endowed with things that the rest of our fellowship lacks; not everything is supposed to be about us, after all.

In Scripture, it becomes clear that when the Holy Spirit helps us, a sense that we belong to the people of God is impressed upon us. John speaks of this in today's reading; Paul emphasizes it too in his letters. For example, in Romans (5:1) we read of the peace with God that we have in Jesus. We wouldn't expect anything less from writers who took earlier Scripture seriously, with its emphasis on the covenant relationship between God and Israel, the people of God.

We need our sisters and brothers, and it's together with them that we study, pray, worship, and help others. This speaks of us being together with others in the family of God. We are not simply a collection of individuals; instead, we are equipped by the Spirit so that we can live out the good relationships that please Him. We have to admit that all too often these days, we fall well below this standard, sometimes expressing hostility and rage towards those with whom we disagree. How can we please God like this?

The Greek word Koinonia was used by those who believed in Jesus in order to describe this sense of being together in God. It means more than merely a working relationship, the term's original meaning. It also implies something more than simple friendship. This kind of fellowship speaks of us sharing in God's life, and we don't do that as individuals with a D-I-Y spirituality. Let's ask the Holy Spirit to make us more aware of others and their needs. As we do this, we can live out what it means to be part of God's people. Only together can we really become more like Jesus who came to serve rather than be served.

Gifts

Read Acts 2:14-21

God calls us to study Scripture with prayerful intelligence. When we do this, with God's help, we become mature and well-rounded characters. We are then able to relate to our brothers and sisters around us in line with the love of God. Then, when it comes to what we believe and do, we can live as those who are convinced that God's Word must to be central in all things (Psalm 119:105).

In addition to this, we read, in today's passage, that those who believe in Jesus were being guided by the Holy Spirit in quite a direct way. In Acts 2 we encounter Peter explaining to the crowd that this kind of thing was made possible because the Spirit had been poured out upon them, as the Prophet Joel had foreseen. For example, the content of some of the dreams that people received would be nothing less than God guiding His people, giving direct and specific help.

The belief that God had equipped His people in this way was widespread following the death and Resurrection of Jesus. Indeed it was written about by Paul in 1 Corinthians 12 and 14. As we mentioned at the outset, none of this is intended to make a sensible and prayerful study of the Scriptures unnecessary. Quite the reverse; it would be by the light of God's Word that the use of these gifts would be measured.

Almost certainly, if we have been believers for a number of years, we will already have experienced some of this for ourselves. It is a normal and natural part of life. For example, God sometimes makes us aware that someone is particularly sad, even if they tell us they are O.K. On other occasions we might have a sense that danger would follow if a particular decision were to be made.

It is right and proper that we use whatever gifts the Holy Spirit has given us. However, we will always need to have an even higher view of all that God has said definitively in Scripture. Alongside this, we will also need to be sensible and wise in all we do. Then, our brothers and sisters can be helped through this kind of ministry, when we allow the Holy Spirit to guide us.

Ministries

Read Ephesians 4:7-16

It's important for any organization to fire on all cylinders. When it fails to do so, it's grievously hampered in performing its task. God's people are no different in that respect. Too few doing too much for too long, damages all concerned; it also saddens the Holy Spirit.

In Ephesians 4, a healthy picture of our life together is given. God gives particular abilities and talents to each of us. The intention was never that some of us should be active service providers, and the rest of us should be those who passively receive what our more gifted brothers and sisters provide. This kind of distortion of what God intends can be widespread, it has to be said.

Whatever God has gifted us to do, the intention is that, as we serve, this strengthens our brothers and sisters and helps them to flourish and use their gifts too. This is only likely to happen, however, when we resist the temptation to defend our patch when we feel insecure. When we feel defensive, we assume that we have value only because we do certain things. If others with similar gifts are also active and excellent, they can be a threat to us. Turf wars follow.

Jesus wants us to grow in maturity and in the sense of security that spiritual maturity gives. He can help us see others as a blessing, not a threat; the One who has gifted them, has gifted us too. When we all do what the Holy Spirit enables us to do, we are happy to take our place alongside others, and everyone feels the benefit. When we are genuinely open to the Spirit of God, turf wars are out, and a godly ministry amongst us all takes their place to the glory of God.

THE FRUIT OF THE SPIRIT

Growing God's Nature

Read Galatians 5:22-23 and Mark's Gospel 9:2-8

It isn't that the Holy Spirit gives us abilities so that God can simply use us. For those of us who believe in Jesus, something much more wonderful than this is going on. The nature of God is actually being grown within us.

In 2 Peter (1:4) we read that we are partakers in the divine nature. This is a stunning truth. God's love for you and me is so wonderful. It is right for us to be amazed at the privilege that is ours. We are invited to delight in God in prayer and worship and to be warmed and changed by the rays of God's love. The good news is that unlike the time we spend trying to get that perfect tan, there can be no harmful effects.

God lives within us so that this can happen, and that's why Jesus sent the Spirit to us. If this were not the case, we could easily end up simply working for a God who is far away. Our calling is much more wonderful than that. The account of the Transfiguration in Mark's Gospel (9:2-13) doesn't only tell us wonderful things about Jesus. It also tells us wonderful things about ourselves and what we are becoming as our human lives glow more and more with God's glory. This is our calling.

Paul tells us, in Galatians, something more about what happens when the Spirit grows God's nature inside us. He describes some of the qualities that flourish within us, as we give God time. These are described as the Spirit's fruit, and like all fruit, it takes time to grow. Let's not be frustrated that it isn't fully formed in us, yet. Let's instead be amazed at what God is doing in you and me.

Love

Read Galatians 5:22-23; I John 4:8; John's Gospel 3:16

Love comes first in the list of divine qualities that Paul gives in Galatians. John spells it out for us, too, when he tells us that God is love. This is expressed fully in the gift of Jesus, the Son of God; it is Jesus who models this divine quality for us. If we want to know what God our Heavenly Father is like, we look at Jesus His Son. We see God's love in Jesus' actions, and we hear about it in His teaching.

It's in order to grow divine love in the hearts and lives of the people of God that the risen Lord sent the Spirit to all who believe in Him. Love really takes shape in us as we give God time in prayer. We also express it in practice in the way we respond to others. This is God's way of helping us to fulfil the Ten Commandments (Exodus 20:1-17; Deuteronomy 5:6-21), as love for God and others grow within us. We find, with God's help, that we naturally want to honour our Creator and Saviour. This covers the first four commandments in this wonderful teaching God gave to Moses. As becoming more loving affects our thinking and the way we act towards others, the other six commandments are kept.

There is effort involved in the Christian life, of course, but we don't make progress in this area simply by trying harder. The important thing is to ask God for the Holy Spirit day by day. From earliest days, believers knew how vital this was. For this reason, the prayer "Come, Holy Spirit," is an ancient one and a very important one, too. As we welcome God's Spirit in prayer day by day, we will find that love takes root in us more and more. God delights to share divine love with us, through the power of the Spirit. This is a prayer God is always happy to answer.

Joy
Read John's Gospel 15:10-11

Joy, for a believer, isn't about becoming an extrovert. Neither is it about becoming loud, or always pretending to be happy. It is about the Holy Spirit within us helping us to rejoice in God whether our circumstances are enjoyable or not. The Spirit brings eternal life to us (John's Gospel 4:13-14). It's a gift, so is the joy we find within us as a result.

Though an emphasis on the importance of joy is one of John's characteristics, it isn't something we only find in his writings in Scripture. It's there throughout the Bible. We read about God bringing joy to Sarah (Genesis 21:6), the Psalms often speak of it (for example Psalm 5:11). In the Prophetic Books, the people of Israel sing and shout with joy to God (Zephaniah 3:14). When Philip preached about

Jesus in a Samaritan town (Acts 8:8), it was natural for them to rejoice, too, for God was active among them.

At the outset, we mentioned about rejoicing in God regardless of the fact that our circumstances themselves might not be enjoyable at all. The Letter to the Philippians is a great example of this. Paul found himself in prison and didn't know what tomorrow would bring, yet there's hardly a book in the Bible with more references to God's people rejoicing than this one.

When we read Scripture regularly, a picture begins to emerge for us, of a God who loves us, is looking for ways to bless us, and is graciously active in our lives. What's not to rejoice in about that? Knowing that we're held in the palm of God's hand and that nothing can separate us from His love means that rejoicing is a natural response. We can enjoy being the people that God made us, filled with the joy He gives. Let's enjoy our Creator who saves us and gives us new life.

Peace
Read Philippians 4:6-7

Yesterday we mentioned about Paul rejoicing in God even though he was in prison and in considerable danger. Today's reading tells us something else about how he responded to his circumstances. He advised the Philippians to pray rather than to worry, then they would experience the peace of God.

Prayer and worry are mutually exclusive; we can devote ourselves to one or the other. Prayer is obviously the more creative choice. It allows us to focus on God rather than on ourselves and how we feel about our circumstances. We'd be wrong if we imagined that prayer always takes our difficulties away. What it does is help us to see everything in the light of the One who grows peace within us.

Peace is a positive quality; it isn't simply the absence of anxiety. To describe it, the Jewish people use the Hebrew word Shalom. The word describes wholeness and wellbeing. It says so much about God and about us in Him.

Believers in some Denominations express their oneness with God and one another as they share God's peace when celebrating communion together. This is far more than merely an opportunity to wander around the church and say "Hi" to friends or to ask them what happened on their favourite soap the night before. Sharing the words "Peace be with you" can be a recognition that the wellbeing of God is finding a home inside us thanks to the Spirit of Christ.

In a world like ours, God's profound inner peace is worth celebrating. Turbulent people can't share peace with others, and turbulent groups can't bring real wholeness to our world. The Holy Spirit, however, can help us to have a positive effect on those around us and on our world. Peace can't really be known in all its fullness any other way.

Patience

Read Philippians 4:12-14 and Psalm 84:1-2

Our world isn't very good at patience. Not many people are given awards because they have this quality in abundance. Quite the reverse, many courses are offered, these days, on assertiveness. This is because we often want to believe that we can get what we want, just when we want it, as long as we learn the technique. How often this is expressed in street demonstrations: "What do we want…? When do we want it? Now!" Waiting is taken as weakness, and we often admire those with the power to get things done, even if others get mangled in the process.

Being passive and letting things roll over us aren't qualities God wants to grow within us, of course. Patience is, however, because this speaks of God's nature. He has a profound sense of inner wellbeing and perfect wholeness; He is also happy to play the long game. We will be likely to have patience when we have a healthy view of God, delight in His presence and make choices in the light of it.

Scripture tells us that God, the Holy One, is unrivalled and has no equal. Even if we don't understand certain things that happen to us, we can rely on the truth that God is Sovereign and delights in us. Today's reading springs from this conviction. It is therefore reasonable for us to know that God works everything together for the best and can be relied on (Romans 8:28). We can live with a real sense of contentment (Philippians 4:12) when this picture of God governs our thinking and our decision making.

It is unreasonable to be patient when we need something and the person who will supply it is either negligent or malicious. Our God is neither. His timescale may not always match ours, but we can live with an abundance of the divine quality of patience when our view of God is healthy. So many in our world are desperate to see it lived out, and we are those who are called to model it.

Kindness
Read Hosea 11:8-9

Today's reading is startling. In a sense it shows us the heart of God. It speaks of the intensity of God's desire to help and bless His people Israel even when they have turned away from their Creator and Saviour. The Psalmist speaks of God being like a loving parent; the children know the kindness that can only come from the Most High (Psalm 103:13).

Jesus heard the Scriptures read in the synagogue Sabbath by Sabbath. How well He understood His Father's nature as a result. The miracles of which we read in the Gospels reflect the intense compassion of the heart of God. In Matthew's Gospel (14:14) we are told of our Lord's compassion for the people, as a result of which He healed those who were ill.

Now, of course, we are intended to believe that our God has compassion for us. We are also intended to experience it for ourselves in daily life. From time to time we meet people who have an unhealthy picture of God, as an angry somewhat unhinged deity who tries to get even with people. We are called to model a much more healthy view and live this out in practice. In 1 Peter 2:3, Psalm 34:8 is quoted; those who were to receive this Letter have already tasted the kindness of God.

Do we really believe that God has an overwhelming desire to bless us? We are intended to. The truth of this needs to take root within us and produce its fruit. How important it is to reject any attempt to paint our generous Provider as miserly or overcome by an irrational type of anger. God is overcome, instead, by an intense desire to be kind to us in practice.

It is good for us to speak to one another quite naturally, and without embarrassment, about the ways we experience the kindness of God day by day. We can also demonstrate this quality in the way we treat others. How can we do this today?

Generosity
Read 1 Timothy 6:17-19

There's nothing wrong with money. There are huge problems, however, with attempting to find security in money, or anything else, rather than in God. It's also unnecessary, for in today's reading we discover that God is generous towards believers. As we receive all we need from God, the fruit of generosity defines how we should be with others. We don't give to charities because of guilt; we give because in being generous, we reflect the nature of God. He is generous not miserly after all.

Many centuries before 1 Timothy was written, the children of Israel, the people of God, were in Exile. Understandably, they wanted to return to their own land, Israel, and some false prophets were suggesting that they would be there before long. But God's message to them (Jeremiah 29:7) was different. They were told that they would be in Exile for quite some time to come. They were left in no doubt that it was God who had sent them there because of their intentional and sustained rebellion against Him. They were encouraged to seek the welfare of their new setting. Seeking the welfare of others speaks powerfully of God's nature. Being miserly and tight fisted are wrong. All too often, this also fails to give us security. And always, being stingy gives a false impression to others of who God is.

In another prophetic book, Malachi (3:10), God's people were urged to be open handed in how they supported the Temple in Jerusalem. If they were, they'd be able to receive God's overflowing blessing. Indeed, Paul emphasises this also in Philippians 4:19. But it's difficult to receive anything when our own hands and hearts are clamped shut.

The fruit that the Spirit is growing within us helps us to be more open to God and aware of the needs of others. When we are generous with money and time in God's work, and in how we respond to others, we are saying good and positive things about God to those who live around us. This is also a good platform from which to speak about our faith in a God who is good to know.

Faithfulness
Read 2 Timothy 2:13

It's in God's nature to be faithful. Psalm 136 drives the message home. In each of its twenty-six verses, the worshipper is invited to affirm that God's faithfulness is everlasting; we can depend on it absolutely.

If we were to believe that in certain circumstances God is unfaithful, it would be difficult to have any kind of firm belief about Him at all. We have been looking at various aspects of God's nature over the last few days. We've only been able to do that because our Creator and Saviour is dependable and trustworthy.

God knows that we are all prone to sin. We let Him down, and none of this is a surprise to the One who knows us better than we know ourselves. What kind of God would call people, use them, and then discard them and move onto others? Certainly not the God about whom we read in the Scriptures. Our God's faithfulness is everlasting. We can depend upon it.

The Bible says certain things about God, and who we are in Him. We are on solid ground when we take all of this seriously. The Word Jesus gives us in the Gospels can similarly be accepted as trustworthy and absolutely true. When we build our lives upon what we know of God, we become the fruitful servants Jesus commends in the Parable of the Talents (Matthew's Gospel 25:14-30).

God doesn't say one thing and do another. It is important that we also become the kind of faithful people on whom others can rely. The Holy Spirit can help us to become increasingly trustworthy and truthful in our dealings with others.

Gentleness

Read Hosea 11:1-4 and Isaiah 40:9-11

God is immensely powerful. We refer to Him as Almighty to affirm this. At the beginning of the Bible, we read that God's awesome power was used for a good and positive purpose in creating all things. When we speak of the gentleness of God, we are not speaking of weakness, but of God's ability to achieve good things by His power. It is this powerful and creative quality which the Spirit grows in us.

There's nothing wimpish about God, and there needs to be nothing wimpish about the people of God either. God's gentle love is powerful, and today's two readings speak of it. The love of God is strong enough to carry the returning exiles: they needed what God could supply. We begin to understand this aspect of God's nature when we realize something of the awesome power of our Sovereign God and the desire that puts His resources at the disposal of the people of God.

Jesus modelled it for us (Matthew's Gospel 19:13-15) in His rebuke to the disciples as they tried to prevent children coming to Him; Jesus showed His power in enabling the weak to receive from Him, then the Lord blessed them and went on His way.

We see this kind of thing in practice when a parent bends down to help a child in distress. This is powerful love coming down to size in order to do the appropriate thing for someone in need. Help can be given precisely because the one giving it is powerful and uses their ability appropriately. A desire to help without the strength to deliver it is utterly useless; and power used in an inappropriate way is terrifying and bullies others. This has no place in the lives of the people of God.

God grows within us this power to act and the strength to do so in a loving way. May this quality describe us as it described the ministry of our Lord. In order for this to be so, Jesus was empowered by the Spirit, and so are we.

Self-Control
Read 2 Timothy 1:3-7

Timothy was called to exercise self-control. This was presumably because, in his timidity, he was somewhat lacking in this area. Perhaps we can be as well.

Lapses in self-control can be highly distressing. Sometimes this can be because of unhelpful patterns of behaviour which make it overwhelmingly likely that we make bad or damaging decisions. Habits are established and our self-esteem plummets as a result.

It isn't that a lack of self-control doesn't matter. It does. Neither is it that God can't help us to make progress in areas in which we are, at present, tightly bound. He can help, and He does. His love for us, and acceptance of us, however, do not depend on having "arrived" in this particular area of life.

We don't always love others perfectly; we recognize that fact, yet we know that the Spirit is growing divine love within us. We are not always perfectly peaceful; again we know this, and the fact that the Spirit's work continues within us. We don't beat ourselves up for not having arrived when it comes to the spiritual fruit of love or peace. Fruit does indeed take time to grow. By the same token, we recognize that self-control may also only arrive completely sometime in the future. This isn't a cop out. It isn't meant to be. But it is an affirmation that the spiritual fruit of self-control also takes time, and that self-esteem depends upon what God is doing within us, rather than how we feel about ourselves at any given moment.

The Spirit of God forms the divine quality of self-control within us when we welcome His ministry. Let's thank God for every sign of the emergence of self-control. What the Spirit has begun will be brought to completion in us. We are called saints; that's a fact. Holiness, or saintliness, might indeed remain a work in progress for us, but its eventual completion is guaranteed. And in God, we have every reason to have a positive view of ourselves in the meantime.

WORSHIP

Three Persons, One God

Read Ephesians 3:14-19

There is something very striking about the Russian Orthodox icon of the Blessed Trinity by Rublev. If you have seen it, you will have noticed that the three Persons are gathered around a table, one on the far side, and one each on the left and the right.

In Eastern Orthodoxy, icons are meant to be prayed over, not simply admired as art. What becomes clear, as we reflect on the mystery of God being three Persons yet one God, as in this icon, is that we are on the near side of the table and are being drawn further and further into the life of God.

Worship is about experiencing the rays of God's love. As we focus on God and worship in the mystery of His presence, we become more and more like our Creator, Saviour, and Life-giver (2 Peter 1:4). The Eastern Orthodox Church often speaks of being changed in this way as Theosis, from the Greek word Theos for God.

Spending time in worship is so important for us. We are called to stand in awe before the mystery of God. When we do this day by day in our homes, as we reflect prayerfully on the Scriptures, we are not solitary individuals seeking the presence of God. We worship as those who share the Spirit of God with our brothers and sisters, wherever they are. Together with them, we are able to delight in Him.

As we daily celebrate the presence of our glorious God, Father, Son and Holy Spirit, we come to know something of the strength the Spirit gives. There is no greater privilege than to be able to offer thanksgiving for the fact that Jesus is at home within us, as today's reading explains. Let's enjoy the presence of God. As we do, we'll become more and more like Him.

The Beauty of God

Read Song of Songs 1:1-3, Psalm 84:1-2, and Psalm 27:4

King David, who wrote Psalm 27, clearly enjoyed being in the presence of God. He longed to spend time in God's tent, the Tabernacle, and when he did, his fears subsided. In a similar way, when worship becomes part of our pattern of life, we look forward to spending time in adoration. When we do this, we are part of a great crowd of people over the centuries who have made time to gaze upon the beauty of God.

There is something very intimate about worship, as God's people delight in Him. This is implied in the language of the Book of Revelation (19:7) in which His people are ready for marriage with the Lamb, the Lamb being a word John often uses to refer to Jesus.

Those who have taught about worship in times past have also made use of the language of love in the Song of Songs, though the book was originally written to celebrate our created sexuality. For some this book speaks of God's faithful covenant love for Israel. For others it indicates the love of Jesus for those who love Him. When this collection of love poems is used as part of our praise of God, however, it can only deepen our encounter with the One whose love exceeds the words we use.

It is this sense of standing before the beauty of God that is often expressed in some of the best worship songs which are now widely used throughout the church. These take their place alongside our more well-known hymns of praise precisely to encourage us to pause in adoration. Our worship is enriched when we gaze at God in this way, and the truth dawns that our God looks back at us in joy. Let's never doubt that truth.

The Victory of God
Read Ephesians 6:10-20

Some stained-glass windows describe a particularly wonderful truth about Jesus. They show the Risen Lord who has clearly won a victory over sin, death, and hell, and shares this victory with us.

This belief stands behind the picture of Jesus that we find towards the beginning of the Book of Revelation (1:12-20). He had died but was shown to be alive forever more: out of His mouth came the two-edged sword of the Word of God. It is this victorious Saviour who stands in the midst of the company of His people, represented by the seven golden lamp-stands. There's something wonderfully Jewish and Scriptural about the words John uses here to describe Jesus.

In the light of these descriptions of Him, we realise that we live in His power, a power which speaks to us of the victory which God has won over sin, death, and hell, as we noted above. Obviously, this isn't an invitation to be arrogant, abrasive, or unwise. It does mean, however, that we are called to see our difficulties and problems in the light of the One who wants to help us and has the power to deliver that help.

When we worship we often see our problems with a sense of proportion. If we are not called to be triumphalistic, we are certainly not called to be defeatist, either. The picture of the Roman soldier's armour in Ephesians 6 reminds us that God defends us; in the power of God, we are able to achieve things and move forward too. We take all of this into account as we attempt to understand the situation in which we find ourselves as God's people at the beginning of the Twenty-First Century. There may indeed be issues which confront us. Yet it is important that we remind ourselves that we belong to the risen Jesus, our victorious Lord, as we plan for the future, and face it with absolute confidence in Him.

The Breadth of Worship
Read Acts 3:1-2; 20:7-12

By the time we have been believers for a number of years, we will almost certainly have settled into a particular pattern of worship for ourselves. We will have come to know what we find helpful. There will be the way we sustain a devotional life day by day; there might be particular Bible reading notes we love; we know what Sunday will bring; perhaps once or twice a year we might go on a pilgrimage or to a conference, depending on our spirituality. These are the things we tend to do, and they seem to work for us.

Now, there is nothing wrong with this, far from it, because God's blessing over the years, our spirituality and character type will all have come together to produce it. Let's thank God for it. A problem only sets in when we convince ourselves that because God meets with us in a particular way, then the way others worship is unhelpful or downright wrong if they prefer something different.

When we read the opening chapters of Acts, the picture which emerges is of a fast-moving and rather bewildering community. Believers will have worshipped God in a huge variety of ways. He was worshipped through the prayers at the Temple; the Sabbath will have been celebrated by most, but perhaps not by all; bread will have been broken on Sunday mornings before people got on with an ordinary day of work; teaching will have been given for hours at a time; others will have met for worship in people's homes (Philemon 2). There will have been much more besides.

It isn't that when it comes to worship we should end up believing that anything goes. It might be good, however, to broaden our own patterns of worship from time to time. When we step beyond the things we like, we are often surprised to find that God can be worshipped in other ways too, and this can encourage us. When we allow God to lead us gently into other ways of worship, this can often be a good thing.

Past, Present, and Future
Read Exodus 15:1-3, Psalm 99:1-2, Psalm 1

Worship really should be about God. Perhaps that's stating the obvious, but sometimes we can end up making it all about ourselves. If worship makes us feel good, it was good. If we felt the same at the end of it as we did at the beginning, we say we didn't get anything from it. The danger of all of this is clear enough. This is group therapy not worship. When it really is worship, it's about God receiving praise and thanksgiving, for He deserves nothing less.

Worship isn't just about "now" either. If we make it all about now, we lose perspective and end up measuring everything by today's certainties. Our readings remind us that when we praise God properly it says something about the past, the present, and the future. God has done certain things, so we thank Him for the created world, the call of our ancestors in the faith, like Abraham and Sarah, the rescue of Israel from slavery in Egypt, the gift of God's teaching to Moses, the life and ministry of Jesus, His sacrificial death and resurrection, and the sending of the Spirit. All these things anchor us and are important in themselves. In the light of these, we can see what God is doing now in the present. Then there are also the things we are taught, and find in Scripture, about what God will do in the future (Romans 8:18-19).

Though worship isn't principally about us, when we focus on God properly, we do benefit from it. Worship gives us stability in a world in which instability seems so widespread; it delivers us from our obsession with ourselves, and helps us think of others; it gives us a confidence that we are held in the palm of God's hand. When we stand before God in heaven, worship will be our chief delight. Let's continue to make it a priority now.

THE JOURNEY OF FAITH

Beginnings

Read Matthew's Gospel 3:13-17

All journeys begin somewhere, including journeys of faith. Around two thousand years ago in the Land of Israel, spiritual washing was often used by the people of God to indicate a real desire to set out on a journey which would take God seriously. For example, a community of people lived together on the shores of the Dead Sea; an immersion in water marked a person's desire to join them. Immersion in flowing water, or living water, could also be used to indicate that someone who wasn't Jewish wanted to join Israel, the people of God.

It was against this background that a prophet named John, the cousin of Jesus, called people to be washed to show that they wanted to set out on a particular journey with God. This would be one which would have forgiveness for sin as its beginning.

The ministry of Jesus would soon begin. Before that could commence, He asked John to immerse Him in flowing water, as His life was entering a decisive and new chapter. It comes as no surprise that Jesus' disciples would also immerse those who wanted to set out on their own journey of faith, as part of their response to His teaching.

For us as believers, we joined the people of God when we received Jesus by faith and showed it by a decisive spiritual washing in water; our journey of faith began. The importance of this shouldn't be minimized. In the turbulent times the Reformer Martin Luther faced 500 years ago, he would often remind himself that he had been baptized. This, for him, announced that he knew himself to be forgiven by Jesus his Lord and Saviour; baptism spoke to him of what God had already done in his life. When we face our times of difficulty and hardship, we can also remind ourselves that we are on the journey of faith because we belong to the people of God. We belong to Jesus knowing that our Heavenly Father has called us to the life of faith. We will live it in the power of His Spirit.

Throughout the rest of our lives, we will go on being blessed and helped by God. This is because we are people of faith who have celebrated the fact with immersion in water. We can thank Him for all that He has already done for us. We know that we can continue our journey in the strength His Spirit gives. He will never let us down.

Moving On
Read 1 John 2:24-28

On any journey, starting well is important, but there can be times later on when we need to decide to redouble our efforts. This is especially the case with the journey of faith which can take a lifetime. It is often in teenage years that we take the faith we were taught by our parents and make it our own. We will need a more mature faith if the journey is to continue through adulthood.

In some churches, a public affirmation, or confirmation, of personal faith provides an opportunity to do this. The renewal of an earlier commitment to Jesus takes place as the Holy Spirit is invited to come upon us once more so that our journey with Jesus can continue. In other churches this sense of commitment to Christ, for the years ahead, is expressed in believers' baptism. Whatever the particular pattern of our local fellowship might be, it is important that we benefit from times of spiritual recommitment through life.

In the Scriptures, oil, which speaks of God's Spirit, can be particularly significant. We read that people are anointed with it when they prepare to do things that God has asked them to do. In 1 Samuel 16:13 David was anointed because God had decided that he would one day rule Israel as King. The help of the Spirit of God would be needed if he was going to be able to do this.

Jesus had a special ministry to perform as the Messiah. We read that when He was washed by His cousin John, the Spirit came upon Him so that His public ministry could soon begin (Matthew's Gospel 3:16). The word "Messiah" means "Anointed One," from the Hebrew word Mashiach. If God's Son needed the Spirit's help in order to be effective for our Heavenly Father, how much more do we?

Because we are in Jesus the Messiah, the Spirit comes to live within us (1 John 2:27). In this way we are given all the help we need so that we can follow in the footsteps of the Lord and be equipped for the task at hand. In the Spirit's strength, the journey continues (Philippians 3:14)

Food for the Journey
Read 1 Corinthians 11:23-27

Paul wrote to the believers at Corinth, in Greece. He needed to because their life together there was so chaotic. When they met to eat, and to bless bread and wine, there seemed little chance that they were really celebrating Jesus at all. Their so-called celebration was more likely to wound their brothers and sisters in the family of God, rather than give food for the journey of faith.

In the Jewish community, within which Jesus lived and ministered, meals were important. They had a spiritual content that Western fast food tends not to have. Families would meet and eat together, in order to thank God for things. The Passover meal was particularly significant for Jesus, as the people of God gave thanks for their rescue from slavery in Egypt centuries earlier. The Passover had always been, for them, a celebration of the salvation only God could give.

From earliest times, those who believed in Jesus ate together and gave thanks for the gift of salvation. This was central when they blessed bread and wine. Jesus had promised to be with them always, especially when they remembered Him in this way. God's intention through this time of thanksgiving was to give the believer food for the journey of faith.

It's as we are strengthened in this way that we understand something of the sacrificial death and resurrection of Jesus. If it weren't for these central truths in our faith, we couldn't be the people of God at all, and Jesus couldn't walk with us day by day. In fact, we celebrate these truths together because we know Jesus Himself to be the Way. Our journey isn't any old journey. On this journey we have a Companion, and He guarantees that we will reach our joyful destination. He will keep us safe until we do. And we can certainly rely on that.

Mishaps and Wrong Turnings
Read James 5:13-15

What's the postcode? It's a sensible question these days when we plan a journey. Many of us use Sat Nav because it's easy to get lost on intersections that are busy, confusing, and unfamiliar. The journey of faith is also not without its puzzling wrong turns.

Leviticus chapters 4 and 5 contain information about how sinful wrong turnings were dealt with in the teaching that God gave to Moses and the people of Israel. Sin can happen for all sorts of reasons. Sometimes we can be negligent; sometimes we can harbour wrong attitudes toward others; we can even become careless in our relationship with God and start thinking that the journey is more trouble than it's worth. When we end up sinning, how good it is to know that with God there is a way back. God can again lead us in the right path (Psalm 23:3).

As we pray daily, we have an opportunity to confess our sins to God. James reminds us, however, that sometimes we need to talk with others about all of this, though confidentially of course. A friend who's spiritual and doesn't blab can be such a blessing at these times.

It can be a real encouragement to hear a brother or sister remind us about God's grace and His acceptance of us. This gives us an opportunity to be prayed for, and it can leave us feeling immensely grateful to God for new beginnings and fresh starts. We are not meant to stagger on, on our own, weighed down by the things we've said, thought, and done over the years, though the devil would be thrilled if we did.

Perhaps today we can make decisions to get our spiritual life back on track. God has promised to lead us in the right way. In that regard, today can be an important day on our journey of faith. Something said or done in the past doesn't need to hamper our future.

Injuries and Disappointments
Read James 5:16-20

Some of the knocks we pick up through life happen when we take a wrong turn—walking down that path was never going to be a good idea, but at the time we wouldn't be told. Some of the wounds and injuries that happen to us as we travel, however, are inflicted by others on their detours; these hurt too. Other aches and pains we pick up aren't our fault, or anyone else's for that matter; bad practice and too much exertion can bring their own stress and strain.

God isn't indifferent to any of this. Neither is He some kind of celestial slave driver: "Stop whining. Put your back into it." God cares about the things that happen to us on the way (1 Peter 5:7). It's for this reason that James talks about the times when God wants to help us through the prayer ministry of other believers. At these times, the use of anointing oil can be helpful.

In the Scriptures, olive oil speaks of the Spirit empowering us for the task at hand. In ancient Israel, it also spoke of healing. In the Parable Jesus told about the Good Samaritan (Luke's Gospel 10:29-37), oil was poured on the wounds of the one who had been attacked and left for dead as he journeyed (verse 34).

When we pick up hurts and injuries along the way, and don't get them dealt with, they make journeying difficult. Sometimes they can even make us feel like giving up altogether. Making sensible decisions about our injuries and disappointments, and allowing God to help and heal us, might be something we need to do right at this moment. We might have carried some things for far too long. When we ask for God's help, we're never disappointed. He's always there to help us, to heal and to bless. So let's allow Him to minister to us.

Various Callings
Read 2 Timothy 1:6 and Ephesians 5:21

We are all equally valuable to God. We are all on the journey of faith, as members of the people of God. In our relationships, and in the things we do and say, we find God's blessing, and we walk with joy along the road He has stretched out before us.

The verses we read today speak of various callings that are sometimes ours on the journey—the callings of serving one another in the family of God, and of marriage.

We are all involved in the mission and ministry of Jesus because we belong to the people of God through faith. We have been washed spiritually in water and we noted how often Martin Luther gave thanks to God for the fact he had been baptised. The truth is that none of us are second class when it comes to being a believer on the journey of faith; we all receive His gifts, blessing and callings. If our particular calling is to be involved in the leadership of the people of God, in this too we can know the blessing and grace only He can give. We don't serve Him in our own strength, whatever He has called us to do in His name.

We are all involved in the life of the family of God and are called to be a blessing in the families within which we live. We do so whether our calling is to be single or married. Single people are a vital part of all our families and enrich the lives of others as only single people can. When our calling is be married, in this again we know the blessing and grace of God to fulfil our calling.

Let's be thankful for the ministries and relationships we have all received from the hand of God. His grace gives us everything we need to live in line with our calling. The One who inspires each of us to live the life of faith will help us every step of the way.

GOD IS....

God is Good

Read Psalm 23

Many years ago, the New York rabbi Harold Kushner wrote a book called When Bad Things Happen to Good People. To read an excerpt from it, visit http://www.myjewishlearning.com and click on Questions of life... Suffering & Evil. In a world like ours, bad things happen; we can't deny that. The Book of Job in the Bible wrestles with the problem of bad things happening when we affirm that God is good.

In Psalm 23, King David looks at this side of life and describes it as walking through a dark valley. In this situation, his response, and the response of people of faith through the centuries, is to affirm that God is there with him and that He is good. David is certain that he will experience God's goodness as he journeys through life. The book of Daniel (3:17-18) makes that basic affirmation of trust in God, and it does so with an appropriate note of defiance towards evil: others might turn to idolatry, but Daniel's friends will never do so.

Believing in the goodness of God is the foundation on which a life of faith can be built. Who would want to trust in a Creator who didn't show basic goodwill toward Creation?

Nevertheless, some of the times of difficulty we go through can seem pretty dark to us. It would be wrong for God's people to make light of things like natural disasters, human wickedness in general, and the Holocaust in particular. Perhaps even now we might be struggling with malice and betrayal in work, from friends or from family members. Feeling bleak can be a normal and natural response to these things.

It's as we go through experiences that almost defy words, however, that we can experience something of the goodness of God. When we don't see the complete picture, He does. Let's not forget that we don't only affirm God to be our Creator; we also know Him to be our Saviour and Vindicator (Psalm 37:5-6). That being so, it makes good sense to go on trusting in the One who, as Sovereign, always has the final word. God is good after all, and that's true now and always.

God is a God of Grace
Read John's Gospel 1:12-14

We looked yesterday at people of faith affirming that God is good, now and always. It is in the light of this that we know Him to be a God of grace.

This belief is rooted in the Psalms: God's people experienced it for themselves and thanked Him for it. We see this worked out in the Gospels as well. The teaching of Jesus shows God's grace to us, and it is expressed in the healings He performed. Indeed, John tells us that Jesus, the Son of God, is "full of grace."

We know that this is how God is in Himself, and this is how He is towards us. That being true, it tells us something about how His people are called to be with others. We can't receive mercy from God by His grace and then refuse to show it to those who have offended or hurt us.

When someone has gone out of their way to wrong us, God doesn't expect us to have warm, fuzzy feelings towards them. Being merciful doesn't ask this of us. We show mercy when we decide not to seek revenge. It is a decision we make. We decide, instead, to treat others as if they had never behaved badly toward us. So our tone of voice remains the same. What we say and do toward them remain unaltered too. In this way we decide to take this part of God's nature seriously.

Not everyone in a world like ours would treat others as we are called to; the phrase "don't get mad, get even" shows us that. But God's grace can sometimes turn someone's life around as they receive this kind of response from us. It can even affect a friend who looks on and sees us treat someone else like this. God is a God of grace. He is also merciful, and He is delighted when we are too.

God Is Holy and Glorious
Read Revelation 4:6-11

The language that we find in the book of Revelation is larger than life. It gives us pictures of our holy and glorious God enthroned in heaven. John frequently calls upon material written in the Scriptures of ancient Israel in order to describe God. Revelation chapter 4 echoes what the Prophet Isaiah said of God as he worshipped the Holy One of Israel in the Temple in Jerusalem (Isaiah chapter 6).

John was on the Roman prison island of Patmos when he had these visions about God and about Jesus, the Lamb of God. In Revelation 1:9-11 he explains that he was consigned to this prison colony as a one of the leaders of God's people because of his commitment to Jesus, the Word of God. This happened at a time when things were taking a worrying turn for believers throughout the Roman Empire. Decades earlier, those who looked to Jesus had seen the Empire as God's way of securing a peaceful and orderly way of life for them (Romans 13:1-7; 1 Timothy 2:1-2). As storm clouds gathered later on, however, Rome started to be seen by them as "Babylon" (1 Peter 5:13; Revelation 14:8); for believers with a Jewish background, who had the highest regard for Israel's Scriptures, this was not a compliment.

Our glorious God rules and is the source of all authority in our world. It is for this reason that we pray for those who are in power. We thank God for Heads of State and Heads of Government when they rule well. When they make life hard for their people, however, we pray for those who suffer at their hands.

Like John, we also remind ourselves that unlike human nations, God's rule will never come to an end. It is in the light of this that we look upon bad leaders in their pride as they briefly strut across the stage of international affairs. How good it is to know the One who is the beginning and end of all things; the love our holy God has for us never comes to an end (Psalm 136).

God Is Love

Read 1 John 4:7-12 and 1 Corinthians 13

The word "love" means all sorts of things to all sorts of people. Various Rock songs might use the word in one way, and poems might in quite another. In today's reading, John describes what he means when he talks about love. For him, it isn't principally about how we feel towards God; it's about what God has done for us in Jesus the Son of God (1 John 4:10). So God doesn't claim to love us and then not follow through on it. In the life, death, and Resurrection of Jesus, divine love was shown to be a very practical and costly thing indeed. Love is sacrificial after all.

That we love others isn't a claim we make in order to try to make them obey us. In the light of divine love, we see that love is about seeking blessing and life in all its fullness for others, even at our expense. According to John, this is the kind of love that finds its source in God, the One who is love.

Sadly, we don't always find that kind of love in our fellowships; it certainly wasn't found in Corinth. There, worship and the way people used their gifts and talents tended to damage others. When Paul dealt with the issues all of this raised (1 Corinthians 12 and14), he put a chapter (13) about God's kind of love right in the middle, so that the believers there couldn't misunderstand. In effect, he was saying, "If you understood divine love and how it seeks the blessing of others, the fellowship here would be different; so let God's love make you different."

Have we ever used the word "love" in an attempt to get others to do what we wanted? If we have, we certainly need to talk to God about it. Our apology to the person concerned might be required, depending on the circumstances. Even if it isn't possible, we might need to act very differently toward them in the future, in the strength God gives. When we seek the advantage of others and allow them to make decisions with which we don't agree, divine love is finding a home within us.

God Is Light
Read Psalm 27:1-6

Sometimes children tell us that they are frightened of the dark. In some cases, they might insist that the light is left on while they go to sleep. It's when we are surrounded by darkness that we imagine dangers of every conceivable kind lurking in the shadows, under the bed, in the wardrobe. When the light is switched on, whatever frightened us immediately disappears.

Psalm 27 tells us that when God is our light and our strength, fear is banished, foes lose their power. God is light; in Him there is no room for darkness at all (1 John 1:5). Very often, it's in the human imagination, alone, that things are conjured up, and fear is triggered. In this way, we can end up wracked with fear, almost terrified, over things that don't even exist in reality. It is for this reason that "fear" has sometimes been defined as: False Expectations that Appear Real.

It makes a great deal of sense to talk to God about our fears. As we do, they can so often disappear in the light of His love. Thinking prayerfully about passages of Scripture, like the beginning of Psalm 27, can help us see things as they really are in the presence of God's Spirit.

We aren't called to pretend that things never worry us. In prayer, however, as we rest in God, we are given the means of dealing with things that often unsettle us all, as human beings. God is light; it is in His light that our "false expectations" disappear.

God Is Trustworthy
Read 2 Timothy 3:14-17

In today's reading, Timothy was reminded of the things he had been taught from his youth. The teaching he had received was rooted in the Scriptures. The Scriptures are God's Word to the people of God, because they had been inspired or breathed into existence by the Holy Spirit. As such, they were an integral part of what believers would need if they were serious about following God.

The Scriptures spoken about in this passage are what we sometimes refer to as the Old Testament. They are "Old" because they were given to the people of God before the Gospels and Letters (the New Testament) were written. They are not called "Old" in the way we might speak of a pair of shoes being "old"—full of holes and ready for the skip. The Old Testament is ancient, authoritative and to be held in the highest possible regard. These Scriptures shaped the thinking and teaching of Jesus, and He referred to them so often when He taught the people. These Scriptures are useful in guiding and teaching those who believe in Jesus, like Timothy, you, and me.

We cherish and use this part of Scripture because we believe that God is trustworthy. What He said in these pages still rings true for us. Timothy was clearly encouraged to have a high opinion of these writings as well, and to accept as trustworthy what God said in their pages.

Taking the Ten Commandments seriously (Exodus 20:1-17), for example, is a good way of saying that we believe God to be trustworthy and faithful. These are a vitally important part of the Scriptures that Timothy was being encouraged to accept. We can't possibly believe that the Ten Commandments are no longer relevant for the people of God, without damaging our understanding of Him. For those who believe He is trustworthy, the teaching He gives us in the pages of the Old Testament acts like cats' eyes marking a highway along which we drive in safety at night. As our pattern of life embraces Old Testament teaching, we become people who are trustworthy, too, in the things we do and say. When we sit light to this important part of Scripture, we are in danger of embracing unsound teaching delivered by those who present a faulty account of the teaching of Jesus. When our thinking is shaped by these Scriptures, which shaped the teaching of the Lord, we stand on much more solid ground. We are then far less likely to be led into error.

God Is Truth

Read Philippians 4:8; John's Gospel 1:14

Truth was important for the first believers in Jesus. Very often, they argued with one another about what to believe, because truth was crucial. They were not simply selling a religious product in the marketplace of competing spiritualties, they were trying to hammer out what was true, because this said something about God.

In his Gospel, John told those who looked to him for guidance and teaching that Jesus was the embodiment of truth. Paul, too, told those who were in his fellowships to think only about things that were true. This is, surely, what we would expect of those who believed that they were called to live in the light of God's truth (Psalm 25:5).

Now of course, it would be wrong for us to claim that everyone who isn't a Christian is indifferent to truth. The fact is that so many people in our world who wouldn't claim to have faith in God still try to search for truth. Many spend their lives trying to define what is true about a whole range of things, like Science, for example. Because of this, we have an obligation to stand shoulder to shoulder with others when truth is being sought.

It isn't that we are pretending that all roads lead to God, or that everyone ends up in heaven regardless of whether they want to or not. Nevertheless, it is still important, for example, that we stand with historians in trying to discover what happened years ago; we stand with politicians in trying to understand what's happening in our world now; we stand with economists in trying to work out what works in practice and how more and more people can enjoy the good things of life.

As believers, we mustn't imagine all sorts of malice and vindictiveness in the heart of non-Christians. When we disagree with historians and politicians, we have a commitment to embrace truth. When we disagree with others in these areas, we have an obligation to use language that is measured and fair. A commitment to truth means that we must avoid maligning and caricaturing others with whom we disagree at all costs. Perhaps even today, we can encourage someone who is being unfairly treated in this way. As we do, the God of all truth stands with us.

ACTS 2:42

The Importance of Being Taught
Read Acts 2:42-47 and Psalm 119:105-112

Toward the end of Acts 2, we're given something of a snapshot of what life was like for some of those who believed in Jesus. Verse 42 shows us the kinds of things that were important to those who lived in Judea before the Good News spread to other parts of the Roman Empire. There were four things that characterized their life. We'll think about these over the next four days.

The first thing was the importance of good, sound teaching. As the chapters unfold in the Acts of the Apostles, we get the impression that a great deal of time was spent by believers trying to understand the Scriptures in line with what they had been taught (20:7-12). This will certainly have been expected by those who had been brought up in the life of the synagogue. For them, sermons would have been delivered, and the Scriptures will have been read Sabbath by Sabbath (Luke 4:16-22).

With the first believers spending time trying to understand all of this, we need to underline that this is something we should take seriously too. Almost certainly, simply hearing a sermon at church on Sunday morning isn't going to be enough to ensure our spiritual health. That's why home study groups, or cell groups, have sprung up in all sorts of churches in recent years. Reading Scripture for ourselves at home day by day is important too.

When we spend time in this way, we understand the Scriptures better. We are also nourished by God in the process and are given what we need to grow in our understanding of Jesus. After all, He was the One who worshipped Sabbath by Sabbath in the synagogue, and grew in His love of the Scriptures. When we spend time trying to understand the Word of God, this is never time wasted.

The Believers Met Together.
Read Acts 2:42-47 and Psalm 133

These days, loneliness can be a real problem for many. This is even the case if we live in cities in which we are surrounded by huge numbers of people.

When we belong to the family of God, loneliness is one of the things we should never experience. We are not on our own. From earliest days, those who trusted in Jesus knew they were part of something much bigger than themselves as individuals. Their shared faith in God their Heavenly Father meant that they were brothers and sisters together.

This, then, was one of the characteristics of those of whom we read in these verses towards the end of Acts 2. Over the centuries, Christians have tried in different ways to express this sense of belonging together in the Lord. Some, for example, have attempted to live together with others in community; the monastic movement, which started in Egypt, grew out of this. Whatever our particular spirituality, we certainly belong together and shouldn't be lone soldiers.

This doesn't mean that we should allow ourselves to be drawn into an intense type of church life which is authoritarian. We fail to reach the level of maturity God wills for us when we allow others to micromanage our lives and dominate us.

Short of this, however, we can know a richness of friendship and fellowship with other believers, which is wholesome and helpful. It can be so good to reach a level of trust with others, which allows us to share our hopes and fears. Often, it is into a quality of fellowship like this that our friends and neighbours can be invited. When we are a healthy community, evangelism can happen quite naturally, even spontaneously.

So often, people are searching for a quality of life which is ours in Jesus the Messiah. Together with our sisters and brothers, we have the privilege of modelling it for others, some of whom will be struggling with crippling loneliness. And that can be just what they need.

The Believers Broke Bread
Read Acts 2:42-47 and Isaiah 40:1-5

The first believers met to be taught the Scriptures and to express their sense of being together. They also met to break bread. In part this refers to eating together, and, as a celebration of the love of God, it was called an Agape, the Greek word which refers to divine love.

As part of their Agape, bread was broken and wine was blessed. Jesus had eaten with His disciples to celebrate the Passover; His followers would later meet, after His Crucifixion and Resurrection, to celebrate all He had done. Acts 2 tells us of the kinds of things they affirmed about Jesus in their teaching, fellowship, and Agape. They believed that Jesus was a Prophet from Nazareth who had performed many signs and miracles; after His death, the Father raised Him from the grave, and His rabbinic disciples were witnesses to the fact. After the Resurrection, He ascended to God's right hand and was known to be Lord and Messiah; He then sent the Holy Spirit upon them as He had promised, in fulfilment of Joel's prophecy (Joel 2:28-29).

Jesus was obviously central in their life together, in their teaching, fellowship, and Agapes. Even though the Sabbath will have continued to be their holy day, the first believers also met to break bread early on Sunday before work, in order to celebrate the Resurrection. As they did this, they knew the Lord to be really present among them, as will generations of Christians after them.

Throughout the church, there are different understandings of how Jesus is really present with His people as bread is broken. The fact is that this and other mysteries will only be fully understood in heaven. The important thing for us, in the meantime, is that we prepare carefully before celebrating our faith in Him at every communion service. As we do, the Lord helps us by His grace. In this way, wherever we are, we celebrate the Risen One as the first believers did in Jerusalem, and our love for Him is deepened.

The Believers Prayed
Read Acts 2:42-47 and Matthew 6:9-15

When we read through Acts, the Letters and the Gospels, we notice that the first believers in Jesus prayed in lots of different ways. However they prayed, prayer was important for them and for their life together in Him, which is why it is mentioned in these verses in Acts 2.

The word "prayer" is like an umbrella term that covers lots of different things. Though the idea isn't that we try to do all of them in a single time of prayer, there is certainly something to be said for this part of our spirituality having a balance to it. In this way, we can know that our experience of prayer is healthy. Otherwise, the danger is that some aspect of it becomes overdeveloped, and that other parts hardly figure at all.

These are some of the ingredients that need to figure in a healthy practice of prayer:-

- Praise: this is when we worship God because of His attributes and qualities. These include His holiness and love. It is good to give praise for some of the descriptions of the Lord we find in the Scriptures, for example, His faithfulness.
- Thanksgiving: we give thanks for the things God has done, is doing, and has promised to do. The Bible and our experience of Him remind us of many things for which thanksgiving would be appropriate.
- Confession: we need to confess our sins to God, in the light of His forgiving grace and mercy. It's best not to begin a prayer time with confession. Initially focussing on God, through praise and thanksgiving, helps to bring balance to our prayers. We confess our sin to Him in the light of an understanding of His character.
- Intercession: we need to pray for others. This is right in itself, and it ensures that prayer includes those we know and those in other parts of the world whom we will never know until we get to Heaven.
- The prayer Jesus taught (the Lord's Prayer): this brings our time of prayer to an appropriate close, and helps to anchor our experience of prayer in His teaching and practice.

Let's make sure we pray each day. As we do, in a balanced and healthy way, our spirituality will grow and develop, and our daily life will be anchored in God.

LIVING THE LIFE

Dare to be Different
Read Matthew's Gospel 5:1-2

Crowds were important to the Gospel writers. They are mentioned so often. We're told that on occasions crowds marvelled at Jesus; sometimes they were divided over what to believe about Him; yet again there were times when they stopped following Him.

As the public teaching ministry of Jesus began, crowds were present. The interesting thing is that Matthew notes that the teaching Jesus gave was principally aimed at His rabbinic disciples rather than the multitudes. The One we encounter, here, isn't "working" the crowds like someone fake and dodgy, but teaching His disciples, seated like the Rabbi He was.

The Sermon on the Mount follows. If you've been to Israel, you might have seen the Church of the Beatitudes near Capernaum and the Sea of Galilee. This is built on the site many believe to have been where Jesus taught. The Sermon describes some of the things we can expect when we live the life God wants us to under the rule of God's love. In a sense, when we take Jesus seriously, we will end up standing out from the crowd because our life choices will be different from those of the crowd.

It isn't that Jesus wants you and me to be narrow and sectarian. He doesn't want us to be disagreeable and quarrelsome in a good cause. These are horrible characteristics in any spirituality. We are meant to be open and welcoming to others. The fact remains, however, that if we receive what Jesus says and live our lives in the light of it, we will be noticed by others, however sensibly and wisely we live.

As we look at the Sermon on the Mount, we'll think together about what it means to live under the loving reign of God, our Sovereign. Through His words, Jesus will invite us to make certain choices and to value certain personal characteristics. He will ask us to take Him seriously. With His help, we can, if we dare to be different from the crowd.

Character
Read Matthew 5:3-12

These verses are amongst the most well known in the Gospels. There's something beautiful and poetic about them. The words we find here describe a particular kind of life, in which we are asked to make choices that will be pleasing to God.

In the Beatitudes, Jesus tells us about the happiness, or blessedness, that is ours when certain things are true of us. The title of this section comes from the word Beatus meaning Blessed as found in a later Latin translation of these verses. It is interesting that Jesus is talking here about the people we are, rather than simply the things we do. The fact is that we will live the life God wants us to when we are people with particular characteristics. In beginning with these, Jesus is getting to the root of the matter.

God's kind of people are humble not arrogant; they have a measure of inner wholeness and are not fractious; they are saddened by things that sadden God; they have a level of self-control and are not overcome and tossed around by an inner rage; they long to see God's will done; they are not deceitful but act with pure motives, and they can rejoice in the security God gives even if they are treated unfairly.

These verses don't give simple answers to the world's complicated problems, much less are they a manifesto, for a manifesto can be championed by all sorts of angry and arrogant people who are dismissive of others. We will live the life Jesus commends when we let God get to work on our character. The message of Jesus in Matthew's Gospel is nothing less than a call to holiness.

A Different Standard
Read Matthew 5:13-16

Jesus started with the character of God's people. The Sermon on the Mount (Matthew chapters 5-7) will go on to give practical advice about the lives we live. Before He gets into this, Jesus tells us, in these verses, about the extent to which our lives will be noticed by others when we live in line with the Scriptures of ancient Israel, as our Heavenly Father wants.

Salt was important in hot climates in days before food could be preserved by being frozen. It was used in an attempt to stop food going bad. In referring to salt, Jesus tells us that our lives are to have the effect of stopping the rot that can sometimes be detected in wider society. We are to make a practical difference. This happens when we don't lose confidence in Jesus, in effect adding too little salt to our lives. When we go to the opposite extreme and react to the world around us by becoming part of a nasty and strident Christian minority, this is useless too. Who on earth would be impressed by food that's been completely obliterated by too much salt?

When we live appropriately and get the balance right, we'll be noticed and have a positive effect on others. Jesus describes this as being like night time lights in Jerusalem, a hilltop city. These are seen for miles around in the darkness. Appropriate living is meant to be like this.

Is God, perhaps, asking us today to make a practical decision that will have a positive effect on others? It could be something as simple as deciding not to gossip about others anymore in a working environment where gossip might be part of the culture. This could say so much about our commitment to Jesus. Certainly it would stop us having a share in people being damaged for the entertainment of others. It would please God too.

The Teaching God Gave
Read Matthew 5:17-20

In these verses Jesus gives a high view of the Law and the Prophets, which we refer to as the Old Testament, and the Jewish community calls the Tanakh. He said He had not come to abolish or cancel the teaching we find there but to give an authoritative application of it. Its content would last as long as heaven and earth. He had come, then, to fulfil it, to teach and live it out in practise. Trying to set aside or ignore the Old Testament would be a bad thing, and in trying to do that, we would be certain to misunderstand the teaching of Jesus. When, in the early communities of believers, some were thought to have a low and dismissive attitude towards it, the Jewish Christians, who continued to hold the Old Testament in the highest regard, remembered and cherished these words of Jesus.

In the previous chapter of his Gospel, Matthew gave an account of the temptation of Jesus. There, He parried every attack of the devil with quotations from Deuteronomy; the teaching of Moses settled the matter for Him. Over the next few days we will notice what Jesus meant when He claimed to give the teaching of the Old Testament its complete fulfilment and application.

We will only be in a position to take Jesus' approach seriously when we become familiar with the Old Testament and learn to cherish its contents. There is significant danger in only reading the New Testament when we read the Scriptures each day. Were that to become our established practice, we'd easily end up doing precisely the opposite of Jesus' approach. We certainly couldn't claim His authority for doing such a thing. Along that road, we couldn't claim to be following Jesus either.

We will be taking the practice of Jesus with the seriousness it deserves when we use the Psalms to give God thanks and praise, and when they become the things we pray. The Ten Commandments (Exodus 20:1-17 and Deuteronomy 5:4-21) are to guide us and keep us safe in daily living. Over the next few days we'll see how Jesus approached this material. Other parts of the Scriptures of ancient Israel also repay our study alongside the Gospels and the Letters so that our understanding of God can grow and develop as it should.

As we walk in the footsteps of Jesus in this way, we'll find a good practice on which we can draw throughout our lives. After all, what is important to Jesus must be important to us, too. We can't improve on His life and teaching.

Anger
Read Matthew 5:21-26

On the shores of the Dead Sea, a group of Jewish people lived together in order to try to take God particularly seriously. In doing this, they separated themselves from wider society. It must be said that they had a particularly low view of the religious establishment headquartered in Jerusalem; it seems that they believed the mainstream groups, like the Pharisees and Sadducees, were compromised by worldliness. Some think that John the Baptist had links with this group. If he did, the things he said about members of the religious establishment would make sense.

Within the spectrum of Jewish thinking, Jesus expressed certain criticisms of the Pharisees and Sadducees, too, though His views were very close to those of the Pharisees on things like angels, spirits and the bodily resurrection of the dead. Together with the Pharisees, the Sadducees, and every other section of Jewish society, Jesus will have agreed on the importance of keeping the Commandments. In today's reading, Jesus gives practical advice on how to follow the teaching "You shall not murder" (Exodus 20:13).

Jesus taught His rabbinic disciples how important it was to deal with the anger that sometimes can be such a feature of our thinking and emotions. In effect, He is saying, "If you rightly want to obey the teaching not to murder, deal with your anger and you can be sure you'll never break it." Thus, the Commandment is fulfilled, not set aside or contradicted.

Let's bring to God in prayer the things that tend to make us angry. As we ask Him for help over these issues, we'll be sure that we don't try to love God and hate our brother or sister at the same time (1 John 3:11-24). With Jesus, we can decide not to take the first steps along the road which ultimately leads to murder. In this way we'll be sure to fulfil the Commandment as He taught us.

Adultery

Read Matthew 5:27-32

In today's verses, Jesus shows how we can keep another of the Commandments. In Exodus 20:14 we are taught not to commit adultery. Again, the approach of Jesus is to advise us to deal with the root of the potential problem, namely, the way our thinking can be compromised by lust. We need to remember also, that it isn't only "bad" people who commit adultery; good people, who never intend to hurt those they love, also make extremely costly mistakes as well. That's what can happen when unhelpful thinking leads to unhelpful practice, and then to the breaking of the teaching of Jesus and Moses.

Especially in an area like sex, it's important that we don't read into the Bible something that's not there. Simply because Jesus taught that lust is a dangerous thing, doesn't mean that He also taught that sex itself is a bad thing. Far from it. Later on in Matthew's Gospel (19:4-6) our Lord says that marriage is rooted in a positive view of Creation, and that it is a good thing that the two marriage partners become "one flesh." The teaching of Jesus on these issues is far removed from those, in the Second Century CE, who argued that the soul was divine and the body was disgusting. How crucial it is that we reject any attempt to push that view in God's name.

Jesus also taught about the sacredness of marriage in highlighting the danger of a flippant approach to divorce. Such a thing robbed the wronged wife of the security that came with marriage in the world in which Jesus taught.

The trust we place in our marriage partner is always intended to be a platform on which a good and positive relationship is built. If we have been hurt by rejection or treated harshly in a marriage that has ended in divorce, God doesn't add insult to injury by doing all He can to make us feel guilty. These verses were never intended to have that purpose. The One who has a high view of marriage, has a high view of us too; He draws close to bring help and healing. Let's allow today's reading to bring us reassurance about God's love and acceptance in this area. Let's also continue to embrace a Jewish and Scriptural understanding of these things.

Be Straightforward
Read Matthew 5:33-37

One of the Ten Commandments God gave to Moses speaks of the importance of not misusing the Lord's name (Exodus 20:7). Yet, in the time of the ministry of Jesus, a practice seems to have been established where people tried to convince others of their truthfulness by swearing oaths. To swear "by heaven," "by earth," or "by Jerusalem" was to wrongly use things associated with God. This was to misuse His name, as Jesus saw it, when simple honesty and truthfulness would suffice.

It's important that we take this insight of Jesus with the seriousness it deserves in daily life. God's people need to be known as straightforward and trustworthy in their dealings with others; our Yes and No should count for something in every area of life.

Though there aren't always simple answers to complicated questions, God isn't honoured when we are evasive in our dealings with others. There is a danger that this can convey the impression that we think we are able to be less than honest and get away with it, because we are too clever to be caught. It's far from helpful when believers respond to a question on which, in truth, they have a view, with an answer that begins "Well, it depends what you mean by that." We don't have to play such games in order to speak with kindness and tact.

God's people are also to be known for honesty in business dealings. The rabbis have been right to speak out about this. In the light of Leviticus 19:14, which tells us not to put an obstacle before a blind person, they have argued against benefiting from a purchaser's lack of awareness about something. It isn't right to keep the purchaser of our car or house in the dark about something just because they didn't actually ask the right question. Being technically truthful but largely dishonest can't be an option for the people of God.

Be Merciful
Read Matthew 5:38-42

In the days before Chinook helicopters, it was no small matter for Roman soldiers to get their equipment from one end of the Empire to the other. One way around the problem was for them to be able to compel a person to carry their pack for a mile; after it had been carried for that mile, someone else would then be compelled to take over. A person, therefore, had a right not to carry Roman equipment for more than a mile.

Here, Jesus is asking His people to stand out from the crowd by not clinging to their rights. Carrying a soldier's pack a second mile would be an act of kindness to the person who would have taken over after the first. It is with small acts of kindness like this that a person could be seen to be living under the reign of God's powerful, holy love.

Being more merciful than others has always been a hallmark of God's people, at all their better times. We find this in Exodus too (21:23-25). In the world in which Moses taught, an injured person might attempt to exact any amount of revenge on the one who had caused the injury. Not so amongst the people of God. God's merciful standard would insist that there had to be a limit to what an injured person could seek under the Law. Jesus taught His rabbinic disciples that they would need to reject harsh and unforgiving ways if they aspired to walk with God.

If we have been wronged or injured, it might be right that the Law takes its course—a lawless society can't function after all. How we respond to our situation, however, can say so much about us. God can help us leave a yearning for revenge far behind, if that is where our circumstances have placed us. To become more merciful is possible with the grace God gives and, truth to tell, revenge really is overrated in the long-term.

Prayer for Enemies
Read Matthew 5:43-48

One of the great things about the teaching God gave to Moses in Exodus 20:1-17 is that it shows that our relationship with God affects how we treat others. In today's verses Jesus again underlines that the people of God should never seek revenge when they have been wronged. In so doing, He alludes to Leviticus (19:17-18). Whatever wrongs we have suffered, we are to love our neighbour as we love ourselves.

Again Jesus shows us how we can do this in practice: we are to pray for those who have wronged us. It's impossible to seek revenge from someone for whose blessing we are praying to God. In this way we are to have the same demeanour towards everyone; God sets the standard here. He is the same towards both the righteous and the unrighteous. If this is the standard we use, we'll stand out from the crowd. God, rather than the wider world, or Gentiles, should be our guide. How different the world would be if we could stop wanting bad things to happen to those who have been bad to us.

As the people of God, we are called beyond this, however, as we are taught to seek God's blessing for those who have wronged us. We can't possibly do this relying solely on our own resources, of course. In order to live this kind of life, we'll need all the help that God can give. And He will give it when we ask.

Perhaps today God will make it possible for us to pray for someone in this way for the first time. It might take courage on our part. But as we pray for God's blessing on others, we, ourselves, will also be blessed.

Life is a Catwalk
Read Matthew 6:1-18

Jesus came to fulfil Old Testament teaching completely. He did this by showing how it could be taken seriously and put into practice.

Within the Jewish community of Jesus' time, three biblical practices were recognized as particularly important: almsgiving, prayer, and fasting. Obviously these disciplines could be practiced in order to please God, the One who sees everything. They could also be done to be seen by other people, in order to earn their admiration. Drawing attention to ourselves like this is never a likeable quality in us.

What Jesus asks of us all, here, is that we have pure motives to govern the spiritual things we do. The giving of money to God's work, and to those in need, praying and fasting are all good things in themselves. Our Lord didn't have a low view of any of them, far from it. But even the best practices can be pursued for the wrong reasons, however.

Whatever our character type or Denominational affiliation, it's vitally important that we do things for the best of reasons. Alarm bells ought to ring when we wonder if we are being noticed by others. God can fine tune our conscience, if we ask, so that we root out from our spiritual practice any desire to draw attention to ourselves. When we do things over the years because we love God, and are moved by the plight of others, the desire to draw attention to ourselves diminishes. Our spiritual practice will then be genuine and done for the right reasons. And that will thrill the heart of our Heavenly Father who sees what we do in secret. Life isn't a catwalk after all.

Anxiety
Read Matthew's Gospel 6:19-34

We are told these days that levels of personal debt have never been higher. This has much to do with in store campaigns to promote credit cards, and T.V. adverts for loans and consolidation loans. In the light of this, we can hardly be surprised at the high levels of personal anxiety we see in society these days.

In today's reading, Jesus taught about a life that is free from anxiety. The key to this was to have a healthy view of God as our generous Provider. Jesus' hearers were invited to put our Heavenly Father first in their lives and have treasure in heaven. To live in this way would give freedom from trying to find security in money alone. It's never a great idea to trust in our own ability and resources and leave God out of the picture.

It's interesting that Jesus also links trust in our generous God with our generosity to others. The writer David H. Stern, in his book The Jewish New Testament Commentary, tells us that in Judaism, the words "good eye" refer to generosity, and "bad eye" refer to meanness. The logic of Jesus is clear: anxiety and generosity to others are mutually exclusive; being convinced that God is generous makes all the difference.

As we started to look at the Sermon on the Mount, we noticed that to live life in line with Jesus' words would make us stand out from the crowd. This is certainly true of the things we are looking at today. So many people who are weighed down by anxiety need to see a different kind of life modelled for them. We don't live a distinctive life because we think we are on the moral high ground and want others to admire us. Far from it. We live like this because Jesus shows a better way, and it's open to all. God is generous to us. Let's be generous to others. In the process, we also have an opportunity to pray for those whose lives have been ravaged by an addiction to gambling. Our generous, powerful Provider and Saviour is able to make all the difference.

How We Treat Others

Read Matthew 7:1-14

Towards the end of Matthew 6 we find that Jesus invites us to be generous to others financially. At the beginning of chapter 7 we discover that He asks us to show generosity of spirit to others as well.

A harsh and unforgiving heart leads us to judge those around us in a harsh and unforgiving way. All we can see are what we perceive to be the faults of other people. When this kind of attitude poisons our minds, it poisons our conversations too. It is also extremely unwise, for when we get things wrong, and we all do, we are inviting others to use this standard to condemn us.

Generosity, financially, becomes possible when we are convinced of the practical generosity of God. Generosity of spirit towards others becomes possible when we are convinced of the mercy and grace He offers us.

When we are on the receiving end of such immense mercy from God, we begin to see the need to treat others in the same way. A much-read book in the time of Jesus, the Book of Tobit, taught that it is important not to do to others things we would hate to have done to us (4:15). Our Lord echoes this and, perhaps, asks us to go beyond it and to treat others in a positive and generous way. We fulfil the Scriptures God gave to Moses and the Prophets when we do this.

Do we tend to be harsh and unforgiving? It takes a lot of courage to admit it if we are. If we recognize that we tend to be like this, however, God can help us as we pray about it. In prayer we can delight in His mercy. When we do, we'll find that the way we treat others begins to change.

Belief and Practice
Read Matthew 7:15-29

One of the things about which I know very little is rowing. But even I have noticed, however, that when two people are rowing well, there is a high level of coordination between them. Both are doing what is necessary in order that the desired effect can be achieved. Attempting to pull in opposite directions can be disastrous, and at the very least, we just keep going round in circles.

If our lives are to have the desired effect, there has to be a level of harmony between what we believe and do. Believing one set of things, and attempting to do something different over a long period of time, could never produce a positive outcome. It is for this reason that Jesus taught that stability in life can only come when our beliefs and practice are in harmony; we can't believe in Him privately and try to hide the fact from others in the way we live.

When we trust Jesus and live in the light of His teaching, we are able to handle what life brings our way. It isn't that setbacks and disappointment don't affect believers at all. The truth is, however, that our faith can make all the difference to us when we are rowing through choppy waters. It gives us something from which we can draw strength in times of difficulty.

Jesus didn't tell His disciples that life would be easy. But He did promise to be with them always. As we walk daily with Him and live in the light of His words, we'll have an inner peace that nothing can take away. We could never rely on better advice than the teaching of Jesus. We will please God as we take it seriously, and we'll be able to live in the light of it in the strength the Holy Spirit gives.

SEEKING AND FINDING

Extravagance
Read Matthew 13:1-9

In Matthew's Gospel (26:6-13) the story is told of a woman who poured expensive ointment over the head of Jesus as He shared a meal with others in Bethany, near Jerusalem. What an extravagant gesture. Jesus was delighted with her action, though some of those at the table with Him were less than happy.

An action like this only becomes possible when Jesus means everything to us. If we only operate on a level that sees our faith as being useful to society, it will be hard for us to understand what this woman did. It would all look just like a huge waste of money. But her great gift expressed her great love for Him.

We find Jesus in a significant way when we seek Him seriously, even if others imagine that our devotion to Him is unacceptably extravagant. We look for God in this kind of way, because this says something to us about His nature and how wonderful He is towards us.

The Parable of the Sower shows us an illustration of extravagance too, depicting something of the generosity of God. His actions take place on the big stage and happen in a big way. There's nothing penny-pinching or miserly about the living God. And we certainly won't respond to Him properly when we seek Him in a small way.

Of course, we need to make sure that no one takes advantage of our willingness to love God in a costly way like this. In every area of life there are those with less than honourable motives. That said, today's reading invites us to take Jesus seriously and give to Him all we have. When we seek in this way, we will be sure to find and to experience the extravagant love God has for us.

Restoration

Read Romans 5:15-17

In the Gospels and Letters of the New Testament we find a certain interest in the future and how our belief in Jesus prepares us to face it. Indeed, that's important. But this can easily drown out another theme in the Bible, namely, turning back to the first pages of Genesis in order to understand Jesus and our life in Him. This is important, too, because the first five books in the Bible were so highly valued by Jesus and the whole of the Jewish community.

In line with this, in Romans we find Paul comparing the bad things that happen to people because of the sin of Adam, with the good things that happen to us because of Jesus. Under the title "the Easter Anthems," this is one of the things we sometimes find in prayer books when a collection of verses from Paul is used to illustrate important truths for us. The idea in this is that God restores everything that Adam damaged, and that this restoration happens in Jesus, the Second Adam.

We will live under the reign of God's love when we become like little children (1 John 2:1) who have been born again by the Holy Spirit of God (John's Gospel 3:5). Seeking God like little children means having a sense of wonder about our experience of God's love in Jesus. We rejoice with gladness and delight in Him with the singleness of purpose a child often has.

Jesus invites us to seek Him and to receive from Him (Matthew's Gospel 7:7). This tells us that we largely tend to receive things from God when we truly seek Him. Let's take every opportunity to seek with a real sense of joy for all of the great things we have already received and will go on receiving. The way we seek determines the things we'll find.

Understanding

Read John 1:1-5

We have a desire to understand God better. This is good. If we didn't, we would hardly spend time praying and studying God's Word.

The truth is that we move on in our understanding of our Heavenly Father when we take Jesus seriously. It isn't simply that Jesus can help us find God's light, but that He is light. Throughout John's Gospel we find the invitation to see Jesus as the One who is central to our experience of God our Heavenly Father. This is reflected in the sayings of Jesus which begin with the words "I am."

When we move on in our understanding and experience of God, we often do this with a real sense of joy (1 John 1:4). In Colossians 1:15-20 we discover that all things were created through Jesus and for Him. Do we have a sense that our lives were designed to give pleasure to Jesus the Messiah? The truth is that we were created through Him and for Him. How wonderful this is.

When we understand that truth and live in the light of it, this can give our lives real meaning and purpose. Our hopes and plans can, in a sense, have "Jesus" written all over them. We are of value to God. He is the One who created us; He is our destiny; He has the final word over everything in our lives, and that is meant to be good news. Let's live as the children of God, clothed in royal robes from the Holy Spirit. We'll do so when Jesus means everything to us.

A SELECTION OF PRAYERS

We call upon the Holy Spirit

Come, Spirit for holiness,
Come, Spirit for power,
Come, Spirit for faith,
Come, Spirit for peace,
Come, Spirit for light,
Come, Spirit for love,
Come, Spirit for truth,
Come, Spirit for joy,
Come, Holy Spirit, come.

God above us,
God beside us,
God within us,
You welcome us,
And we declare Your praise.
Blessed be God, Father, Son and Holy Spirit.

In praise of Jesus

Blessed are You,
Jesus, our Ruler, our Saviour.
In You we see, enfleshed,
The true image
Of the brightness and glory
Of the living God;
You are to be adored.

We marvel at Your likeness
Taking shape
In the lives of
Your many sisters and brothers
By Your Spirit;
The Word becomes flesh, even in us,
And You are to be worshipped.

Blessed are You,
Jesus, our Ruler, our Saviour
To the glory of the living God.

God grows His Nature within us

Spirit of God:
You are the fountain
Pouring forth abundant life,
Yet You are never diminished;

You proceed from the living God,
By stages growing the nature of God
In dry and thirsty human hearts.
Sent by the only-begotten Son,
You clothe the children of God
In royal robes.
You surround us with the peace
That only You can bring,
And purify our hearts with Your refining fire.
We delight in Your holy presence,
Spirit of God.

Surrounded by God

Almighty God, You are here and everywhere,
You are the One in whom we rejoice.
Help us to live today as those who are
Aware of Your encircling presence.

Living with Jesus

You overshadow us, our Protector;
You uphold us, our Rock;
You go before us, our Guide;
You walk behind us, our Defender;
You refresh us, our Living Water;
You nourish us, our Bread from heaven;

You teach us, our Word from God;
You scatter our darkness, our Light in this world.
You are all we need, and You care for all;
You are beyond us and within us.
Glory to You, Jesus our faithful Messiah.

From glory to glory

Holy One, Breath of God,
You are perfect and complete.
Yourself needing nothing,
You meet all our needs.
You set us free,
And in You
The children of the Second Adam
Live forever.
Give us faith to receive You
And love to share You.
Come, Holy Spirit, and transform us,
From glory to glory.

A Prayer of Commitment to God, based on the Ten Commandments.

You are our God, the Living One,
From Whose hand we receive freedom;

We will never replace You with anything;
We will never reduce You to what our
Minds can comprehend;

We will never use You for our own
Selfish purposes;

We will celebrate the holiness of the Sabbath,
And delight in this day of rest.
We will keep our work in its proper place,
With a due sense of proportion;

We will honour our parents,
Those who care for us,
And those who lead us,
That we may continue to know Your blessing;

We will honour life as Your gift,
For You are the Life-giver;

We will not sin with others,
But will honour those we love with faithfulness,
For You are faithful to us and to all;

We will not take what rightfully
Belongs to another;

We will not attempt to harm our neighbour
With lies and deceit;
We will be truthful in our dealings with everyone;

We will not show ingratitude to You,
Our generous Provider,
By begrudging others Your gracious gifts.

Help us to love You and others completely;
Help us to rejoice in Your teaching;

Empower us by Your Spirit, we pray,
That we might live before You
In line with the example of Jesus, our Saviour,
And so bring glory to You, our Sovereign.
Blessed be God, Father, Son and Holy Spirit. Amen.

BIBLIOGRAPHY.

The Authorized Version. Cambridge University Press.

The New King James Version. Nelson. 1988.

The Third Millennium Bible (New Authorized Version). Deuel. 1998.

The New International Version. The International Bible Society. 1984.

The Revised English Bible. Oxford University Press, Cambridge University Press. 1989.

The New Revised Standard Version. Division of Christian Education of the National Council of the Churches of Christ in the USA. 1989.

The Tanakh. The Jewish Publication Society. 1985.

The Jewish Study Bible. Ed. Adele Berlin and Marc Zvi Brettler. Oxford University Press. 2004.

The Complete Jewish Bible. JNTP 1998.

The Jewish New Testament Commentary. David H. Stern. JNTP. 1992.

The Authorized Daily Prayer Book of the United Hebrew Congregations of the Commonwealth. Fourth Edition. 2007. Collins, London.

Forms of Prayer for Jewish Worship, volume 1. 1977. Reform Judaism, London.

Siddur Lev Chadash. 1995. Liberal Judaism, London.

Principles of Jewish Spirituality. Sara Isaacson. Thorsons. 1999.

Judaism—a Short Introduction. Lavinia and Dan Cohn Sherbok. Oneworld, Oxford. 1997.

Judaism—a Short History. Lavinia and Dan Cohn Sherbok. Oneworld, Oxford. 1994.

Israel—a History. Martin Gilbert. Black Swan. 1999.

http://www.myjewishlearning.com/ideas_belief/sufferingevil.htm

Prayer Book – In Accordance With the Tradition of the Eastern Orthodox Church –
All Saints of Alaska. Kindle Edition.

The Septuagint – translated Sir Lancelot C.L. Brenton. Kindle Edition.

The Tanakh. The Jewish Publication Society 1917. Kindle Edition.

Also by Martyn Perry:

Wisdom for Living Volume 2

Also found on Amazon

Printed in Great Britain
by Amazon